I DEDICATE THIS TO,

all of the confused, lonely, out of touch, not quite sure, anxious, happy, afraid, in love, heartbroken, lost but finding their way, right where they want to be but not quite there yets.
I was and still am one of you.

#FEELS

table of contents

#FEELS

table of contents

introduction

WHAT IS ONE TO DO WITH ALL OF THESE #FEELS?

A question I've honestly asked myself many times whether I lay pitifully on the floor with mascara smudged down my cheeks or was on top of the world beaming ear to ear as I struggled to absorb as much of that blissful state of happiness as I could. In a matter of minutes, hours, days, and weeks we can feel everything from complete misery to elated euphoria, and it makes sense. We are the most blessed and messed up generation on this planet. We are one giant adorable mess (only not all that adorable if we're being honest). We have access to so much yet connect with so little. We have limitless potential yet lack self-esteem. And for this reason I decided to write #feels.

Now don't get me wrong, I don't believe I am the all-knowing wise One with the ability to cure all the #feels that course through our veins. That said, I have spent many days and nights puzzled by confusion, paralyzed by loneliness, overwhelmed with anxiety, jumping with excitement, buzzing with inspiration along with many other intense feelings. To no surprise, I found myself struggling with the idea of how to navigate through it all. There have been so many times that I've had to sit down and write out a pep talk to anchor my focus or talk myself out of the darker sides of life. I used to pray for a magic formula to pop up on my screen as I frantically searched Google for ways to calm myself down in a middle of a panic attack or work through the mean little voice in my head that told me I wasn't good enough to accomplish my dreams. This is ultimately what led to the creation of #feels.

Consider this little book to be your own personal pep talk through all the #feels we work through on this crazy train we call Life. A guide to all of the terrible to the magnificent, the mean to the mundane, and the impossible to the intense. Within these pages you will find solutions - from how to overcome your past, be at peace with your present and manifest your future. It will be your go-to guide that you can open on your phone in times of panic, darkness, or pure bliss. It will help you work through your relationship with yourself, your life, and everyone else around you. Lastly, it will leave you with some game changers so you can set yourself back on the right path or help you further along if you feel you're already heading that way. Ultimately, it's like having a best friend in your pocket. It is as if I am tucked inside of your phone, sipping my decaf coffee, and snapping my fingers sayin' "Oh no he didn't" whenever you need me.

As much as I wish we could all have someone on speed dial for all of the personal pep talks this life requires, this is what I leave you with instead.

introduction

So, I'm curious. How do you #feel?

Flip back to the table of contents, locate what you're feeling, and let's start sappily pep talking ourselves back together so we can leave our ugly cries as a thing of the past. **You've got this.**

PAST, PRESENT, FUTURE

05

#FEEL 1

I WISH I WAS ANYWHERE ELSE

So, your mind is wandering off to a million other places or moments you wish you were instead of right here in this second. Maybe you're laying in your bed miserable, maybe your life feels like it's falling apart, or maybe nothing is even going that wrong, but you wish that it was more right. You dream of living it up surrounded by friends in California, or meeting your soulmate traveling through the streets of Tuscany, but instead here you are, reading this book looking for the fastest way to escape to anywhere but here.

I have some good news and I have some bad news. Let's get the worst part out of the way. You can't just snap your fingers, click your heels, and vanish to a place or time far from now where you're happy and things are different. Look around you, this is where you are. This is one of the many milestones and stepping stones of your life that is leading you to whatever destination you want it to lead to. Whether you do want to be eating your way through Italy, or even jump into another life completely, this right here is what you have got to work with. This is your starting point. That's the bad news, which to be honest, isn't even that bad. You have total control in becoming inspired by this moment. If there's even a tiny part of you that wishes to be anywhere else, it means that something is not adding up in your life. That doesn't mean you have to run away or hide from it, it means it's time to take what you've got and start making something out of it. Grab those lemons and make that lemonade or slice them up and take them with tequila shots, whatever tickles your fancy.

#FEELI

I wish I could sit here and tell you some magical way to escape your life, but not only would it be pure nonsense, it would also be a shame. You are here for a reason; you have been given this life, these circumstances and this time and you can create something huge with it. The ugly and the pretty is yours for the taking and you can make of it whatever you want. It would be a giant waste of time to dream of escaping to anywhere else because without the work and effort it takes to change your circumstances and actually end up somewhere you want to be, the same old problems would continue to follow you.

So, ask yourself, if this isn't what you want, what's missing? Is it a place to call home, people to love and support, a beach view from your kitchen, or a heart to hold in your hands and a set to give your own to? Whatever it is, write it down. If you could be anywhere but here, where would you be? What would it look like? Who would you be around? Now take a step back and look around you. Take it all in. This can either be a means of your misery, or a stepping stone to a place in your life where you no longer dream of being anywhere else. I know it would be so much easier to give up all control and responsibility for where you are now, but why put yourself through that when you can easily shift your perspective and try to find the light in your current situation. Regardless of what you decide to do, time is going to pass, and you can stay exactly where you are, feeling exactly as you do now or you can push for something better. You can decide to find the inspiration and gratitude for this moment knowing it's a minor barrier or pivotal point that's leading you exactly where you want to be.

You can be grateful for the things around you right now, the age you are, the time it is, for your dogs' constant love and affection that may not always be there, or for the moment you decided to take control and start changing your life. One day you'll look back on this phase of your life and as weird as it sounds, a part of you will miss it no matter how miserable you might feel. So, get up, dust yourself off, stop wasting your time wishing to teleport to anywhere but here, and start making something exactly where you are.

This life has handed you these lemons. Get going on that lemon meringue, those tequila shots, or whatever it is you want to make of these citrus goods. **You've got this.**

#FEEL 2

I'M STILL HURT

Whether it's from someone you love, a circumstance outside your control, or even from yourself, holding onto pain from the past is one of the most paralyzing things we can do to hinder our potential happiness. Here's the thing: every single person on this Earth has been wronged or hurt one time or another. There's nothing that can change what has already happened, but there is a way to change the outcome of it.

Holding onto the pain and wishing for a different outcome is a waste of your time. Instead, try to shift your perspective and see it from a different angle. For one, was there anything this pain brought you? A lesson it taught you? Even if you don't see it now, how can this pain be shaping you to deal with something else in the future, or prepare you with the mental tools to help someone else? There is no denying the validity to the saying "What doesn't kill you makes you stronger". With that, we should stop trying to change the things in the past that hurt us, and instead try to let go of the pain and reap the benefits. I understand that this isn't something you can just snap your fingers and be over with. If there are steps you need to take to get through the pain, take them. Cry it out, feel the pain, write a letter to whoever hurt you and throw it away. Release anything you've kept tucked away and then let go of it completely. Then, write a letter to yourself (or if that feels too cheesy, just simply make a verbal promise to yourself) about how this situation has changed you for the better, what it has taught you, and how you won't let this pain control you or your happiness anymore. Trying to find the positive in any negative is an instant way to feel better about it. If you can make this a habit, you can learn to become one of those annoyingly positive people in any situation, and that's a good person to be.

I'm not saying that you should try and train yourself to never be hurt by anything because the fact that we get hurt is a sign that we loved or cared for something so deeply we allowed ourselves to be vulnerable. Trying to guard or shield ourselves from that would also mean trying to keep ourselves from ever loving or caring for anything again. This would inevitably lead to more pain and a lot of mental rewiring to do in the future. Instead, love openly and care deeply. Trust that the Universe wouldn't put anything in your path that wasn't meant to bless you or teach you a lesson, and always look for the meaning in every event that happens in your life and how it can deepen your character. And lastly, forgive anyone that hurt you. Forgiveness isn't easy but try and put yourself in their shoes and take a good look around. Is there anything that could be going on within them that makes them hurt other people, or is there a chance they didn't mean any harm at all? When we forgive the people who hurt us, we don't just let them off the hook, we free ourselves from the heavy weights that holding onto resentment brings.

(A whole #feel on forgiveness is on page 141, just saying)

GAUTAMA BUDDHA

"What you think, you become. What you feel, you attract. What you imagine, you create."

#FEEL 3

I'M AFRAID THE PAST WILL REPEAT ITSELF

When we fear the past, we let it control our present and predict our future. Letting go of the things that haunt us is one thing, but to find a way to not let it paralyze us in fear of repeating itself is a whole other ball game. Even when we feel as though we've healed from past experiences, there can still be a part of us that tries to guard ourselves from it happening again, whether it be getting heartbroken, failing at something we love, embarrassing ourselves, the list can go on. The thing we don't realize is that this fear and the precautionary measures we take to protect ourselves from it tends to attract more of the thing we're so afraid of. If you've flipped to this page, there must be something that you're terrified of happening to you again. Pull it up in your mind. Sit with it and feel the emotions it brings to you.

Now ask yourself, has this emotion that it stirs from you created any action or thought in your mind that may be controlling you? Are you not fully going for it for fear you may fail? Are you not putting yourself out there again in fear you may get hurt? Are you not forgiving your past because you don't think you've really changed?

We may not realize it, but even after the healing has happened and we're long gone from the moments that may have hurt us the most, we still let so much of our past experiences control our lives and hold us back from the things we want the most. You can't waste your precious time here on earth worrying about the things that have already happened to you, or worse, worrying that they may happen again. This will only attract more worry and fear into your life allowing more not-so-great things to happen to you as you constantly act out of defense. Instead, look at what that moment in your life may have taught you. How has it made you the person you are today? What did that pain or problem show you about what you truly want for your future?

We must ask ourselves these questions to re-anchor our focus. Shift the weight from fear of the past to excitement and faith in the future. Trust that the Universe placed that learning lesson on you in order to shed light on something you may have needed to learn and move forward with the knowledge it taught you to a brighter future. I'm not saying completely forget about it, but anytime that fear creeps its way into your mind, stop it dead in its tracks and remind yourself of all the amazing things you are currently working towards, even if you can't see them yet.

The thing about our future is that we have no idea what shape it may be, and while that might be terrifying, it can also be exciting. It's like driving down a long highway at night but only being able to see the few feet of pavement ahead of you lit up by your headlights. Sure, we can predict the next few days, weeks, or possibly even months of our lives, but when we make those predictions from a place of fear and worry we only attract more fear and worry into reality. If we instead predict from a place of self-confidence and faith, we take the tiniest bit of control we do have back and attract more self-assuring proof that we are destined for the greatness we desire.

Never, ever be ashamed or afraid of your past because it made you exactly who you are today and prepared you for everything you'll need tomorrow. You are exactly where you are meant to be. Just trust yourself and trust the Universe and you'll never have to fear history repeating itself again.

CHUCK PALAHNIUK

"You realize that our mistrust of the future makes it hard to give up the past."

13

#FEEL 4

I REGRET MY DECISION

Regret – much like the fear of our past repeating itself, it's one of those mental prisons we hold ourselves in despite the fact that we have the key to freedom. If there is one rule you can ingrain deep into the pits of your mind about life, let it be this;
we are destined to make mistakes.

If we didn't make mistakes, how would we ever learn? Holding onto regret about a decision you made or the outcome it presented gives you the illusion that you could have controlled or manipulated your life to result in another outcome. If you knew then what you know now, would you have chosen differently? Perhaps, but there may come a time when you'll look back on the thing you regret most and realize it was a pivotal point in your life that brought you exactly where you wanted to be, or better yet, a life so amazing you could have never seen it coming.

For starters, if you're regretting something that once made you happy, then let that shit go. You cannot beat yourself up for giving yourself something you wanted in the moment, whether it was downing an entire pizza or devoting your time to the bad boy you had a hunch would break your heart. Sometimes in life, we do things even though somewhere inside we know isn't good for us.

#FEEL4

Why? Either there is something we want to know, a lesson we may need to learn the hard way, or maybe for once we just wanted to throw caution to the wind and indulge life without fear. Why should any of these things be something we regret later?

Here's the thing, without being morbid, the time we have on this Earth is limited. In fact, let's take the average person's life span.

78 years – 365 days – 24 hours – 60 minutes = 40,996,800 minutes.
1,440 minutes per day.

Now with that number sitting in front of you, think of how many minutes of your life that have already passed. Why on Earth would we want to take away from the mere 1,440 minutes we have today, wishing we could change the outcome of the minutes already gone?

#FEEL4

#Feels Game Changer: Jot Journal

Ask yourself this:
1. What are 5 things you want to accomplish in this life?
2. What are a few of the steps it'll take to accomplish these things?
3. What do you want to eat for dinner tonight?
4. Who's someone you love and wish you could speak to right now?
5. What's something you haven't done in awhile that brings you joy?

Do you have these answers strong in your mind? Awesome. Now stop wasting the few minutes you have today regretting the past and instead shift your focus on all the things you could be doing instead. For example, getting back to that mindless task that used to bring you joy like reading, sketching, or rollerblading. Call up that old friend or your sister and talk for hours, or even better, meet up with them for coffee. Head to the grocery store and grab all the ingredients to make your favourite meal. Grab your day planner and start mapping out the tasks that will lead to your dreams and goals in life. Whip out the scissors and tape and collage yourself a dream board. You have no control over what you've already done and the outcome it brought you, but you do have control over what you decide to do right now in this very moment.

You can sit here and spend it regretting the past, or you can see what outcome you can still make of your future. Our time on this Earth is limited and it would be a shame to waste it regretting anything that once brought us joy or left us standing exactly where we are now. We are far too busy living the life we love and working towards the one we want to be making any sort of fuss about regret.

You've got this.

MARSHA PETRIE SUE

"Stay away from what might have been and look at what can be."

17

#FEEL 5

I MISS THOSE DAYS

Pain comes from desire.

Desire comes from not being attached to the present moment but instead living through the past or waiting anxiously for the future. Whether it's missing the life you had a year ago or the feeling of recess and sandboxes from simpler times of being a kid, yearning to go back to that version of you is creating the sadness and emptiness you feel inside yourself now. We can take some of our best memories and want them back so desperately that we paint them in a shade of grey that haunts us daily. The trouble isn't in wanting to go back, the trouble is that you are not in love with your present (to which I suggest #feel 1 – *I Wish I Was Anywhere Else* pg. 6).

Often times we think back on the memories in our lives and instantly want to escape to that moment thinking it's the surrounding circumstances or the people we were with that brought us so much joy. What we don't realize is what we are truly yearning for is the version of ourselves in a point of our lives. What kind of days are making you flip to this #feel? Are they the days of holding hands with someone who you once thought was your everything, but is now just a stranger? Are they the days of peanut butter jelly sandwiches and afternoon drives to the flea market with your grandparents? Were they the days of being in school surrounded by all of your closest friends with your biggest worry being the homework assigned the previous night?

#FEEL5

It could even be a more recent time in your life where you felt everything was aligned; you were accomplishing and doing the things you love, surrounded by people that love you. Now think about those moments deeply. What exactly about them is causing such a deep longing? Most times, it's the happiness we felt in those moments. The way our hearts were full. The person we were, the way we thought, the way we looked at life.

Instead of longing for a moment of the past that is impossible to get back to, why not get wrapped up in the life you have now and all the ways you can generate the same feelings you had then? It's not an easy feat to learn from our past and prepare for our future, all the while staying as present as possible, but it's something we should practice every day. You should get so wrapped up in the chance you have right in front of you to do whatever you will with your life, and then create something so incredible you wouldn't dare escape to a previous time – but do it justice by continuing to carry that joy into days ahead.

Honour your past by living in the present and do everything in your power to be the best and do the best you can. This is the trick to living a fulfilled life.

#FEEL5

#Feels Game Changer: Time Travel Meditation

Get quiet and clear your mind. Picture yourself at the very end of your life, in your later years with grey hair and aged skin from years of smiling and laughing. Make this image vivid, such as how tired you may feel or how your body may not be able to do what it used to. In that mindset, imagine how you might feel if you were greeted with the chance to go back to exactly where you are now. If you were able to go back and be the age you are now, move as you do now, breathe, live, and create as you do now. What things would your older self appreciate if dropped back into this stage of your life? Would it be the family around you? The gift of time to create or start something new? The ability to travel and the adventure waiting just outside your door? Or maybe even the opportunity to cuddle up with your dog on the couch to watch your favorite movie?

Pretend that chance was actually given to you as you carry on through your day. As if that older, close to the end of life version of you was given the chance to wake up today in this phase of your life. Think of how you might make the most out of every precious moment knowing it was all given to you again. You wouldn't yearn for the past, instead, you would be so present in the moment knowing that it was a gift and that your future was promised and showed signs of love and fulfillment.

Any time you feel yourself missing the past, do a quick travel meditation wherever you are to bring you back to the gift of the present.

#FEEL 6

I MISS SOMEONE WHO IS GONE

If you're reading this, I'm sorry. I'm sorry there's someone who has passed away whose loss is leaving you in the state that you're in. Know that missing them is never a waste of time and wishing they were still here isn't a loss of touch with reality. There aren't any words that can be said to fill the part of your heart that belongs to whoever it is that is gone, but there is this: We have no idea what comes of this life. We aren't entirely sure why we're here or what happens next. All we know is what we can see so who's to say the people we've loved and lost aren't in a sense still with us? The memories you've shared, the things they taught you, the sense of home they brought you is still all within. Harvesting on these good feelings of someone who is gone is a way to bring them back to you whenever you need them.

Think of the situation in reverse. If you were gone, how would you want the people you love to live on? Of course, we all need to spend time to grieve the loss, but eventually you would hope the ones who loved you would carry on with living their lives and accomplish great things not only with you in their hearts, but also with you on their mind. I'm not saying you should move on and let go of whoever you've lost because to have loved someone enough to miss them as deeply as you do is a blessing. That said, sometimes the only way to make the people we believe deserved more life on this planet is to use up the rest of our time wisely with their memory as our strength.

#FEEL6

It's alright to be sad. There is no special trick or pep talk out of that #feel, so let yourself feel it. Then tuck that sadness away and shed some light on the positivity the person you lost left you with in this life. Imagine what they would say to you if they were here right now. Imagine the joy it would bring them to know you were happy and living your best life in honour of them, and then live on in that state of mind bringing every little piece of them with you.

PAST,
PRESENT,
FUTURE

23

#FEEL 7

I'M ABOUT TO PANIC

Follow this breathing pattern immediately.

Breathe in 1...2...3...4
Hold 1...2...3...4...5...6...7
Breathe Out 1...2...3...4...5...6...7...8
Repeat.
Also linked here: http://www.duffthepsych.com/stopanxiety

Breathe. There is nothing you need to do, think, or worry about in this moment aside from breathing. There is nothing you can control or change in this moment except for your breath. Zone in and focus on taking care of your body by breathing. You are just having a panic attack, there is no real danger happening to you in this moment. For every thought that tries to cross your mind and bring you back into panic, tell yourself "NO". End the catastrophic thoughts by saying no as loud as you can inside your head or aloud if you are alone. Fight against them and protect yourself against these thoughts. Now reassure yourself. Follow up your "no's" with affirmations like:
"I am exactly where I need to be."
"Everything is happening for me, not to me."
"I am the captain of my seas and the master of my fate."
"I am safe, loved, and cared about."
"There is nothing I need to be worrying about except for myself at this exact moment."

#FEEL7

Once you've found yourself in a calmer state, take some time to reflect. Don't minimize what happened by pushing it away. Instead try to find the moment of emotion that triggers your panic and if you can and feel comfortable enough, explore it. Is there any way you can accept the way you are feeling? Telling yourself it's okay to be exactly where you are, feeling exactly as you do takes away the panic that there is something wrong with you out of the equation. You have all the time in the world, you have all the care in the world, you are not alone, you are not in danger, your mind is just trying to protect you, even if it doesn't seem like it.

Instead of hating your anxiety or getting down on yourself for feeling anxious or panicked, love and appreciate your mind for trying to protect you and give yourself the acceptance it may need for feeling unsure or frightened by the uncomfortable or the unknown. Tell yourself it's okay to be afraid but that there is no immediate danger. Try to look at your situation from another point of view to gain a fresh perspective.

In two weeks how might you feel about it? In two months how might you feel about it? In two years how might you feel about it? The only way out is through it.

One breath at a time, one moment at a time. Breathe into this moment and take care of yourself first.

#FEEL7

#Feels Game Changer: Wise One Meditation

Picture yourself from an outside perspective looking in on your life. Only you have lived through all the lessons of life and seen the outcome of everything that has ever happened to you. Imagine looking in, knowing that you have all the answers this unknowing version of yourself may be seeking from the world, that you are calm and at peace knowing that life is not as serious as it may seem. See yourself struggling with these anxious feelings and feel the love and protection you want to bring to this version of you.

If this is difficult, imagine yourself as a child or even replace the image with someone else you care deeply for. In this state of panic they may be in, what wise words would your all-knowing self give this person or version of you? How would you comfort them knowing they are in a state of need? What affirmations would you tell them so they felt no need to worry? What kind of things would you give them to not only relieve their state of panic but also prevent it in the future? Remind them of how strong they are, of how they have survived every panic attack or anxious feeling before, and how they have so much resilience in them even if they can't see it yet.

ROY T. BENNETT

"It's only after you've stepped outside your comfort zone that you begin to change, grow, and transform."

#FEEL 8

I'M AFRAID OF CHANGE

Change isn't always easy. There is good change – your body after weeks of committing to working out and eating healthy, our habits after kicking the bad and trying the new, our hair after deciding to get a fresh trim or new colour – but there is also some change that we resist and fear. This can be anything from graduating school, growing another year older, accepting the separation of family, or moving away from home. No matter the change, it can still be scary to face the end of a chapter we may have wanted to keep reading, even for just a few moments longer.

If there's anything to learn about change it is this; good or bad, it brings us something. When I look back on changes I resisted and feared, all I see now is the necessity of those changes to bring me to exactly where I am today and morph me into the person I'm becoming. When we get too attached to our comfort zones, anything that may shake it up instantly terrifies us when instead we could be inspired to embrace this new change and see where it may lead us.

Whether it's a change you've decided to make or change that was brought upon you by fate or the Universe, we must let go of what we expect from life and be open to where it's really taking us. I know that's easier said than done but think of this: was there ever a time in the past you were afraid of a new beginning? Maybe it was your first day of high school, the beginning of a relationship, trying out for a new team, or putting yourself out there to chase your dreams. Is there a time you can think of where you were in fear of a new change happening but can now see how needed it was?

Our lives are one linear course. We move down the road and through the phases and seasons of our lives, sometimes unknowingly and other times so aware of these moments we try to stop dead in our tracks. There is no going back or pressing fast forward. There is only here and now. Even this moment right in front of you may be one that you'll fear to let go of. We must embrace and be inspired by the constant changing, not only in our lives but also all around us if we wish to continue to evolve. Even the changes we see as detrimental are a way of the Universe showing us a lesson we may need to know in the future or to setup a better circumstance for yourself or anyone involved down the road.

I'm not saying that the fatal blow of a breakup or the pain of your parents splitting up should leave you grinning ear to ear. What I am saying is that we must learn to stop teasing our minds with the idea that we have any control over these kinds of changes and instead look at them as an opportunity to start fresh again. We need to reinvent ourselves on a daily, weekly, or monthly basis in order to continue growing and adapt to whatever life throws at us. If we can learn to be inspired and become wiser by the changing seasons our souls venture through, we can learn to become invincible to the anxieties that follow with trying to handle and control all these circumstances in our lives. To see the good in any bad change, to find the inspiration in new opportunities set before us and to make all change good change – this is the secret to constantly seeing the world and our lives with fresh eyes.

#FEEL 9

I CAN'T CONCENTRATE

This feeling comes as no surprise. Just think about the reality we live in where our phones are constantly demanding our attention. We can barely complete any task without at least checking our home screen 5-6 times to see if we received any texts, calls, emails, or the accumulation of likes on our most recent Instagram photo. Our mind is constantly in a million places at once, so it's no wonder why we all struggle to concentrate. Amplify this by 1000 if you're stuck on something in your mind from the past (such as how horrible a moment you had yesterday was), or the future (such as how on earth am I going to get all of this done in time so I can get to my hot yoga class by 6pm?).

Zone in, right here and now. Check your surroundings. What time is it? What is the one and only task you should be focusing on right at this moment? If your brain is cluttered with multiple tasks, then the one and only task you should be focusing on right at this moment is making a goddamn list woman (or man), because you are all over the place.

Make a list of all the things you need to get done today. Put a (*) beside the three most important and time sensitive tasks. Pick one of them and that will be the only thing you will focus on for the next 20 minutes. Put your list and phone away, turn off your notifications, and set a 20-minute timer (okay you may need your phone for this, so be sure to turn on airplane mode). For the next 20 minutes, devote your entire mental and physical effort at getting this task done as best as you can. Try to do this without any thought going to anything else you may need to do today or any problem that may be circling your life right now. Just twenty undivided minutes to the task at hand. When the timer goes off, take a five-minute break. Drink some water, check your phone if you must, but after those five minutes end, set another timer and do it again.

It sounds crazy, but we must set aside time not only to work and focus, but also to brainstorm or do things aimlessly. Setting aside not only the 20 minutes of straight work time, but also the 5 minutes of free time will help get your brain back into the pattern of focusing and relaxing. Do this for the entire week and see how much your concentration increases along with your productivity. If you're finding it easier by the end of the week, bump up your focus time to 30 minutes or even an hour.

The only trick is to never go past an hour without at least 10-15 minutes of rest or relax time. Even better, order a timer from Amazon so you don't need to use your phone. Concentration is this sick joke we play on ourselves because we expect to be able to focus from 9am to 5pm. We get so frustrated when we've been at it for hours at a time without any sort of mental rest or recoup. You don't need to get up and leave your seat to give yourself five minutes of aimless thinking and tasks. You just need to have a concentration plan and execute it accordingly.

So, are you ready? Set the time, time to focus.

You've got this.

#FEEL 10

I'M DEPRESSED

You can do this. You are equipped with everything you need to continue to fight through these darker times in order to get back to the brighter ones. From the moment you were placed on this earth you continued to fight against your odds. You learned to walk regardless of how many times you fell, you tried new things despite wanting to run home where it was safe, you made friends despite the fear of being in a new environment, you went back to sleep despite the nightmare you may have had and now here you are. You can't stop fighting now. Your younger self wanted more. You secretly want more.

When we are depressed, we paint everything in a shade of grey. From the moment we wake up, we wish to retreat to that empty space between sleeping and dreaming where you can forget the way your reality rains down on you or how the future is something that no longer holds excitement. We struggle to speak, walk, move, hell we struggle to even shower. We let ourselves go and, in the end, we wind up painting ourselves grey too. What's easy to forget is that we're the ones holding the paintbrush.

You don't have to fix the way you feel overnight, you just have to keep trying. Keep fighting because these demons and this darkness are not who you are, it's just what's haunting you. When we are depressed, we are living in the past. We must pool all of our mental effort together by taking things one task at a time. It's time to get up, it's time to brush off, it's time to give yourself better because it's what you deserve. It's time to make your younger self, that little fighter that's still in you, proud. Everyone on this planet is plagued with some sort of distraught or hardship in their life. Everyone has something that causes turmoil or burdens them in some way. We all carry the weight of our past, but we can put that weight down pound by pound.

Think back to a time that you felt happy. What were you doing?

In my darkest times I do my best to remember when I last felt happiest and recognize the habits and traits I carried during those times. Don't focus on the outside circumstances at that time, circle in on what **you** were doing.

Were you following a routine? Spending more time outside, exercising regularly, giving yourself free time to get creative, working on a project or goal that brought you joy, exploring the world outside your door, exploring the world inside your mind, putting together outfits that made you feel like a rockstar, volunteering or working somewhere that left you with a sense of accomplishment? If you can't think of a time you felt happiest, ask yourself what would it take to get you there? What dream life can you conjure up that brings even the tiniest piece of light to your grey?

You don't have to adopt all of these habits now. You don't need to jump up and run out the door, you just need to try. Fight to try at least one of these things and see if they make you feel any better. When we feel we have no purpose, we are left with an emptiness inside of us. This emptiness can trick us into believing we are worthless, talentless, and that trying at all is a waste of time. But it isn't. If you need a purpose in life, let it be this: to find your joy. To do things that bring you joy no matter how successful they are in the eyes of anyone else. It can be anything from growing a garden, to more ambitious goals like becoming a yoga instructor. Don't deny yourself the one and only chance to live this life exactly as you want to.

This is the time to rid yourself of this emptiness and be there for yourself. To treat yourself as if you are still that younger kid, coaxing them through the hard time they are going through. To take care of yourself in a way that no one else has ever before. When we love ourselves and we let ourselves do the things that brings us joy, we suddenly find a lightness to life that was missing before. Our shades of grey regain colour and we see that life isn't meant to be taken so seriously. We understand that with balance comes highs and lows. That our journey puts us through dark times to pivot us towards something we are destined for and gives us the tools to get there. These times of depression are really just times of rest and rewiring. If you are depressed you are not on the right path so if you must, rest and come up with a plan of how things are going to change. Pivot your life and start painting with light again.

You can do this. You've survived 100% of your worst days. You not only survived, you fought, you learned, and you kept going, so don't stop now. You're on your way.

VIVIAN GREENE

"Life isn't about waiting for the storm to pass, it's about learning how to dance in the rain."

35

#FEEL 11

I'M LONELY

Everyone in their lives, at one point or another, goes through a period of loneliness. Whether you've pulled away from the world in isolation or people just seem a little more distant than usual, loneliness can be an empty feeling that's hard to shake. One thing you should keep in mind: there is a difference between lonely and alone. Instead of focusing on how lonely you feel, try focusing instead on how much you enjoy spending your time alone. When we are fully content and at peace with who we are, we love having time to ourselves.

We learn to love living alone, doing hobbies alone, even eating or going to the movies alone. If you're going through a phase of feeling lonely, it may be the Universe giving you a chance to face your fear of being alone and to learn to love your "you" time. It could be a chance to learn not to rely on other people, to distract you from the things you may not like about yourself, or to fill your time and keep you happy. When we become our own best company, we also become better company to those around us and people naturally begin to gravitate towards us.

So how do we become our own best company? We start treating our alone time as a blessing instead of something we should fear. Think back to when you were a kid. How many hours did you spend running around in a world of your own, so full of life and imagination that you barely noticed anything outside of your bubble? We must learn to re-enter that way of thinking. To get so wrapped up in the things we love that bring us so much joy that we feel full of life all on our own. To fill our time with hobbies, passions, and exploring new interests, we learn the most about ourselves and grow further into our full potential. One day, far off into the future, we might have spouses, children, families, responsibilities, and a long list of other things occupying so much of our time it might be impossible to find a moment to ourselves. In those times we will think back to these moments in life where we were able to just exist on our own, soaking up our time with anything we wished.

So, fill up your planner with "you" time; dress yourself up, take yourself out, try something new, read a book, start a new hobby, do something you've always wanted to do but kept pushing off. One day you'll look back on this phase and realize the strength it brought you and the bond it created within yourself.

#Feels Game Changer: One Week Solo Retreat

Come up with seven different ideas or goals that have peaked your interest at one time or another in the last year. They can be anything from curating a new playlist, making a cookbook, trying a new restaurant, learning an instrument, checking out the bookstore, spending time at a park or with nature, getting into a new exercise regimen, the list goes on. There are an infinite number of things we can do that we haven't given ourselves the chance to before.

For a whole week, schedule one task a day and put your full attention and focus on putting your all into it. Anytime you begin to feel sad or lonely, stop the feeling dead in its tracks and say to yourself or out loud, "I enjoy my own company. Hell yeah, I can't wait to *insert task here*". It will feel weird and corny, but it works I swear.

Keep track of how the week goes in a journal or in your mind each night before you go to bed. Note how you feel at the beginning of the week, during each task, and at the end of each day. Doing this Game Changer will eventually lead you to a new hobby or routine you enjoy doing alone. It could spark a new passion or open up a new opportunity you never thought to explore. Eventually you will get so consumed by your new project or goal that you'll forget the time or date. You'll get so used to enjoying taking yourself out it won't ever be a second thought. With time, you'll become your own best friend.

JEAN-PAUL SARTRE

"If you're lonely when you're alone, you're in bad company."

#FEEL 12

I NEVER WANT THIS MOMENT TO END

Breathe it in. Look around you. Take in all your senses. Where you are, what you're doing, who you're with, how you're feeling. Embrace it and love it without holding on too tightly. Let yourself feel the bliss, let your body soak into the buzz of life surrounding you and take as many mental snapshots as you can. Heck, take actual snapshots if you can. Capture it, date it, bookmark this moment in your mind. Moments like this are the ones that make us.

These are the places we go in our mind when we need to find a happy place in a not-so-happy time. This is the beauty of life. The art of balance. This is the peak to the valley and you should bask in it for as long and as much as you can. Fill yourself with gratitude for the moment, let that energy fill you and spill from your smile and your eyes. Let that light fill your bones and bleed out through your actions and words.

When we are truly happy, when we are so present in the moment that we don't want it to ever end, we can suddenly push ourselves into an anxious mode of trying to hold onto it desperately in fear of it slipping away. This can cause us to believe we live a life of lack instead of abundance. We become defensive and protective of the things around us instead of grateful and giving. Don't let yourself get there. Instead, appreciate this moment for exactly what it is. If we can be grateful and inspired by these moments, we can attract more of them into our reality. When we become appreciative of the small things that make the moments up - just being surrounded by the people we love, the colours of the sky, the perfect song playing at the perfect moment - we train our brains to see the joy of life and shift our default mode to this infectious perspective.

So, soak it in. You are happy. You deserve this. This is life.

#FEEL12

#Feels Game Changer: Mini-Moment Meditation

Take in your surroundings at any chance you can. The time, the place, the people, what you're doing, the colours, the foods. Find a sense of gratitude for five things going on right in this moment. You can do this without anyone around you knowing. This will instantly take you from feeling spaced, disconnected, and mundane to happy and fulfilled any time you need it to.

#FEEL 13

SOMEONE WITH ME IS KILLING MY VIBE

Okay first things first; Can you escape this person? Can you get out of the situation? Can you spend the least amount of time with them as possible? If you can, do it. It is not selfish to distance yourself from anyone who's bringing you down. It's good to remember that anyone who's breeding negativity and treating other people poorly is usually dealing with something within his/herself. We can't control the way people behave towards us but what we can control is how we react to it. It can be hard to not take it personally, but it is imperative to being able to protect our happiness and energy.

If given a situation where you are unable to escape someone who is truly killing your vibe, it's important to get into the right mindset. Is there a reason you know of as to why this person might be upset? Put yourself in their shoes and see if there's anything that could be causing the tension, including anything you could be doing. Is this person worth painting yourself in the same toxic mood or stooping to their level in order to treat them in return for the way they are treating you? I know it's cliché, but we should try to treat others the way we want to be treated. Think of a time where you may not have been in the best mood or were dealing with something that was really difficult. How would you want those around you to react? During those times you don't intend to ruin anyone else's day, you're just hurting.

If we can find sympathy for the people who are treating us wrong, we become unaffected by their behaviours or malicious actions. When we continue to be happy even though someone may be trying to bring us down, we release ourselves from the toxic energy that's threatening to consume us. By doing this, we take away the satisfaction of whoever it is that is throwing the shade. It's been said before so allow me to say it again - kill them with kindness. Let your sympathy be your choice of reaction. Let your happiness be your revenge.

#FEEL 14

I DON'T HAVE ENOUGH TIME

Here's the thing about time, when you tell yourself you don't have enough of it, there will never be enough. I am the queen of believing I don't have enough time. I'll end up procrastinating, spending half the time I say I don't have doing all the things I don't need to be doing, leaving me with no time left to do the things I actually needed to do in the first place. Even worse, it leaves no chance to do anything I'd actually love to spend my time doing either. Sound familiar? Here's how to fix it.

First off, **prioritize**. What are the three most important things that need to get done today? Do those first. Then, what are two things you'd really enjoy doing today? Do those next. If you have any time left over, knock more things off your list. If there's no time left over, sleep well knowing you had a balanced day and completed as much as you could. There's no point in stretching yourself thin trying to complete a million tasks in one day only to half-ass all of them. Take things one task at a time. Be completely present in each task. Suddenly, you'll realize you have more time than you could have ever thought.

#FEEL14

Prioritizing tips:

- Make a to-do list or use an agenda to keep track of what you need to get done.

- Pick the top 5 things that you will get done that day. Three needs, two wants.

- Use a highlighter and place a star next to those five items and forget about the rest until these first five are done.

- Before starting each task, take a minute to fully check in to what you're doing and put your all into it.

- Each night spend 20 minutes coming up with a plan for the following day or each Sunday planning out the next week to keep on top of your time management.

- Wake up 15 minutes earlier each morning, even just to meditate or relax. It will give you the illusion of having more time

#FEEL 15

I DON'T WANT TO BE HERE ANYMORE

Suicide Helpline – 1-800-273-8255

Let me start off by saying I know that anything within this book won't take away your pain. It's a heavy responsibility to write something that may change your mind, so instead I'm going to tell you my experience with this feeling in hopes that it may somehow help. On a foggy October morning, I sat in my computer chair and stared out of the window. So numb that I honestly couldn't tell you how long I was sitting there. I felt so empty and lost but at the same time I felt nothing at all. I remember thinking to myself that I didn't want to exist. I didn't want to be here anymore, I didn't want to wake up tomorrow. I didn't want to have to endure another day in this life or deal with everything it would take for me to ever want to feel alive again. I couldn't see a way out, I couldn't come up with any plan, I couldn't fix the things that had been weighing me down for so long. All I could see was a long narrow path of always feeling this way and dealing with the same things that I couldn't see ever changing. I didn't see myself ever feeling happy again. I just wanted it to all go away.

That led to a downward spiral of thinking of ways I could make it end. I racked through options so easily I almost began laughing at how fucked up it all felt. In fact, I did start laughing. Chuckles filled the air as it hit me how easily I was sifting through ways I could end my life. It was all so dark, that it wasn't long before my laughs turned into sobs. I cried so hard I couldn't breathe. There I was on the floor, curled up into a ball completely wrecked. I knew I didn't want to die but I also knew I couldn't keep living like this. I felt as if i was slowly dying from the inside and it brought me to a point where I began planning my death.

It was then and there that I decided I had to do something. Anything. There had to be more than this. So, I decided to have faith. I chose to believe that one day I would look into the eyes of someone I loved and know that's what I decided to have faith in. That there would be a day I would hold my first child in my arms and know that's what I decided to have faith in. That I would accomplish something amazing or do something I never thought I had in me and know that that's what I decided to have faith in. That there would be a quiet moment on the couch with my kids and my future partner as we watched movies and ate popcorn that would bring me so much fulfillment and know that's what I decided to have faith in. That not only one day, but multiple days in my future I would be hit with this feeling of life, love, and light and know that's what I decided to live for. That even though I felt so empty, so broken, and so lost, I had to have faith that eventually things would change and I would carry my defeated self there on blind faith.

To remind myself of that faith, I got it printed on my arm right where I could see it so when I was weak, I could look down and remind myself there were better times coming. Also, for when those moments were happening - waving my hands in the air at a concert, petting my dog as we watched a movie in our new apartment, holding hands as I said my "I Do's", hugging my children, carrying the groceries in to make a Thanksgiving feast at my home - it would be there to remind me that those were the days I had faith would happen.

No matter where you are in your life right now, no matter how you are feeling, there are days ahead that I promise will make this pain worth something. There are so many moments of pure bliss ahead of you, you just have to keep breathing. Keep fighting. Keep going.

I know it isn't easy and I know it can feel helpless when so many of the reasons we get to a point of not wanting to live anymore are circumstances outside of our control but trust me when I say it gets better. It will all make sense eventually. You will learn to work with the things you can control and let go of the things you can't.

You will learn to love yourself again. You will learn to find the light in any given situation. You have so much strength and life inside of you. You will have a day, if not a thousand where you look back on feeling this way and know the moment you are in is what you decided to live for. For the love you haven't been able to feel yet, for the eyes of your future children, for the hands of those you'll help along your journey, for the moments of pure bliss that will bring tears of joy to your pained eyes.

Please have faith in that. Please have faith in yourself.

You won't always feel this way and if no one else is there to tell you, let me remind you that your life does matter. It matters to me, it matters to you, and we need you here. Seek the help you need, tell someone you're feeling this way, call a helpline, do what you can to survive this storm in your seas but never let your ship sink. You are the captain and no matter the wave, you can ride it out. One day you'll wake up and there will be sun, and it will be because of your storms that you appreciate it's warmth in a way many aren't even capable of.

Have faith. **You've got this.**

PAST,
PRESENT,
FUTURE

50

ELEANOR ROOSEVELT

"Today is the oldest you've ever been, and the youngest you'll ever be again."

51

#FEEL 16

I'M NOT WHERE I WANT TO BE

You may not be where you want to be, but you are exactly where you need to be. We have to trust the journey and the timing of our life or else we will constantly spend it feeling out of control and unfulfilled. You are exactly where you are meant to be. Everything happening to you right now is happening for you. Each and every moment in your life is a stepping stone towards what you are striving for.

If we had the ability to hit the fast-forward button, we would skip past all the character building moments of breakthrough and clarity. Wishing to be at any other point in your life is a waste of your time and energy. Time and energy that you could instead be putting into the moment right in front of you. It's okay to find contentment with your life whilst also working towards something greater. The trick is to have no expectation at any given moment; to not expect at any time, age, or point in our lives to be doing any better or any worse. Instead, take away the expectation and look at what you have to work with right in front of you. How can you make the best of this moment right here? How can this moment catapult you to the place you wish to be? What are things you can be grateful for when it comes to the place you are already in?

If we spend our whole life wishing to skip forward to the things we are working toward, we rob ourselves of the opportunity to be happy in the meantime. We leave ourselves so consumed with wishing to be further along in our journey that we miss the people we love around us aging, the moments we take for granted passing and the memories we'll one day look back on happening right in front of us. We're wishing to skip past time that so many other people would kill to have more of. We stop trusting the timing of the Universe, and with doing so, we take away our ability to be content and happy with the present. This is because we are so overinvested in our future. No matter what it is you are working toward; whether you're in the middle of school, trying to get healthy, at the beginning of manifesting a new goal - appreciate the step you are currently standing on.

Appreciate the things you're currently learning; the time you still have, the ability to snap into the present, and take full appreciation for everyone and everything that is still around you. Your life won't always look like this. Inevitably, time will pass, things will change, people's lives will move along, including yours. It would be a shame to one day wake up and wish to come back to the point of your journey you so badly wanted to skip over. Do yourself a favour by enjoying it now and soaking up as much of it as possible, with the utmost content as you continue to move forward along the timing of your life. If you have the right mindset and align your energy with gratitude and self-assurance, you can sit comfortably exactly where you are, knowing that what you dream of is on its way to you. Patience is key. In the meantime, get up, get out, and enjoy exactly where you are. You will never have this day again.

JOHN LENNON

"Time you enjoy wasting, was not wasted."

54

#FEEL 17

WHAT IF I WASTE MY LIFE?

There is no such thing as a wasted life. Wherever you are, whatever you're doing, it's all part of the bigger picture of your journey. If we constantly worry that anything we do will be the wrong move or a waste in time, we'll find ourselves constantly hesitating before making any sort of decisions leaving our lives stagnant and non-progressive. We can't let the fear of a wasted life paralyze us from moving forward. We instead must lean into whatever feels right in our bones and trust that whatever it is, it'll be exactly what we need right when we need it. If you follow your gut and intuition you will never be led astray. If anything, worrying about a wasted life is a waste of life in itself. Use the time you have now, because the future is never promised.

Are you wasting time now by not going after what you truly want? Are you wasting time now worrying and obsessing over why you're here and what you should be doing, instead of following your bliss and letting it lead the way? Of course there are things we have to do, that is inevitable. We must work to survive, but you can find a career that both supports you and fulfills your passions. We need to do tedious tasks such as cleaning, paying bills, and traveling from point A to point B on any given day. These things are also not a waste of time, in fact they are a part of the balance of life. They are what give us the ability to live our lives comfortably and with a sense of accomplishment. Even the time we spend with no goal in sight, aimlessly walking around outside, or doodling on papers for fun, none of it is waste of time. This is living in its purest form. This is giving your brain space to breathe and be.

What a concept; to just be. Time is an illusion. It is something we invented. When you can think outside the box and realize that these seconds, minutes, hours and days are really just one linear pathway leading you with no visible end in sight, you'll realize there is no waste. It's all part of the adventure. The moments, faces and places are the scenery along our journey. The struggles and problems we face are merely speed bumps along the way. The blessings and unexpected surprises are flowers growing from the concrete. It's not when we finally figure out what we should be doing, where we should be, or who we should be with that will make us eternally happy. Life doesn't stop after those moments. The path keeps moving along and we keep walking. Instead, we must learn to enjoy the journey, trust the path, and realize that all of it feeds the bigger picture of our lives. There is no such thing as wasted time, only wasted energy worrying about the life you have right here and now.

Get walking.

#FEELI7

#Feels Game Changer: 7 Day Wasted Time Challenge

When was the last time you forgot what hour it was? When did you last get so lost in something you forgot what day it was, where you were, or that any of your problems existed?

- If you can think of something, spend 30 minutes a day for the next seven days doing that task.

- If you can't think of anything, think back to things you enjoyed as a child. Some ideas: Drawing, walking, running, driving, listening to music, reading, painting, writing, designing something, building something, trying a new makeup look, starting up a new YouTube, Tumblr or Pinterest page, perfecting a new hobby, or talking to your best friend.

- Keep a log about your change in mood and anxiety each day after the 30 minutes is up.

#FEEL 18

I WON'T FIND LOVE

First of all, this is far from true.

The person you will end up with is out there right now. They could be sitting in Starbucks drinking an order they'll one day have you obsessed with, they could be working away at their job, or at school which will one day be part of the support you both use to build your lives together. They could be looking into the eyes of another person and realizing they are not the one and you're still out there. They could be walking around wondering where the hell you are! Either way, they are out there and they are doing something right at this very moment as you read this page in a state of lonesome #feels.

It's not easy waiting around for the right person to walk into your life, but there is no way to speed up the process. You can put yourself out there, you can go on dates and ask your friends to hook you up with singles they know, but regardless of what you do, the person you will ultimately spend your life with is getting to you as fast as they can. All the meanwhile, you are too, only there is no way to control the how or when this happens. In the meantime, telling yourself you will never find love is only attracting that exact reality to you. When you walk around sulking, feeling as if you are not worthy of being loved or that you'll never find the one, your life will start shifting accordingly only to prove to yourself that what you're saying is true. Saying that we will never find life is a cop out for putting ourselves out there, having faith, and giving it a try. Telling ourselves we are not worthy of love is a whole other ballpark and if that's what you're choosing to believe, then you aren't ready to find love yet (and you should flip to #feel *I'm Not Loved* pg. 115 after this).

What we have to do in these times of waiting is focus on sharpening ourselves up so that when the right person does walk into our lives, we are ready for them. Shift your focus as best as you can on becoming more of who you are, doing the things you love to do, and growing as an individual. There will be a time you look back on your single years and feel a sense of nostalgia for the days you could get lost in your hobbies, jump on the opportunity of trips, or dance all night with your girlfriends as you all wondered what your lives would become 10-15 years from now. So, shake it off, let your loneliness go and start filling up your planner with things you want to do and places you want to visit, people you want to see, and those bucket list items you want to hit.

Keep moving forward and keep building up the other aspects of your life so that when the right person does come to you, you're ready.

(Check out the *Single AF Bucket List* on pg. 120)

#FEEL 19

I DON'T WANT TO GROW UP

The thought of getting older can be scary. What will it be like when our youth is gone? When we have more years behind us than ahead and when lines sketch our faces from years past? If there's one thing we do know it's that ageing is inevitable. No amount of surgeries or money can stop the natural process of life. We have to stop fearing the inevitable and instead find the blessing in it. Think of how many people that weren't able to grow into their elder years. The ones who would give anything to have a few more days, months, or years. Ones who wanted to grow old with the person they loved. Ones who wanted to chase their dreams and retire on their successes. Ones who wanted to start a family and watch it expand before their very eyes. Ones that wanted to share their wisdom learned throughout the years to their children, and their children's children.

Getting old can be a scary thought, but when we see past the superficial fears of it, we're left with the awe and blessing it would be to make it that far in this life. To one day wake up having spent years with someone who can always make you laugh when you're sad. To hear the laugh of your grandchildren on Christmas morning as you serve a feast to your extended family. Heck, to be able to spend your afternoons making your favourite sandwich and sitting on your front porch listening to some old Britney "Hit Me Baby One More Time", reminiscing on the old days while you read something on what will probably be a holographic book. All of our best days are still ahead of us. To grow into the years where our bodies become a little slower, but all while our memories become a lot fuller is a privilege, not a curse.

One day I hope we all get the chance to watch our youth fade, and to have many years full of memories and moments behind us. To have lines sketched into our faces from the smiles and laughs we were blessed with along the way. If there comes a day I'm able to look into the eyes of my grandchildren and share a terrible joke or a bit of wisdom, I will smile and think back to how silly I was sitting in this moment, fearing the day I would ever get such a blessing to live a fulfilled, long life.

C. JOYBELL C.

“We can't be afraid of change. You may feel very secure in the pond that you are in, but if you never venture out of it, you will never know that there is such a thing as an ocean, a sea. Holding onto something that is good for you now, may be the very reason why you don't have something better.”

62

#FEEL 20

I HAVE NO IDEA WHAT TO DO IN LIFE

Ahh, the good old "what the hell should I do with my life?". We can spend years worrying and obsessing over what the perfect career or pathway is for us. We can stress over what job matches best to our personality, what will bring us the most success, what will allow us to have some free time to do what we love, or what we have enough money to study for or invest in. It can become incredibly overwhelming to put so much pressure on one fateful decision. That stress and pressure can become so consuming it blinds us from being able to see the answers right in front of us. What we should do with our life is easy, it's letting it find us that's difficult. Yes, you read that right, letting **it** find **us**.

When you were a kid, you never asked questions, you just did what felt right. You let your inspiration and imagination guide you. Somewhere along the way, we trained ourselves to stop trusting our imagination and our intuition, and instead trust facts and the opinions of others. We have to get back to the child in us. Even if the things we were into then, don't align with who we are now, our way of thinking can still breed many answers to questions some of us spend our whole lives asking.

#Feels Game Changer: Working with the Kid in You

1) Think of things you used to love doing as a child. Were you a collector, a mini fashionista, a tree-hugger, an animal lover, an adventurer, a want-to-be artist, a performer, a leader, a solo go-getter? Sit down and brainstorm as many things you can think of and the characteristics you had.

Now bring these things to the future. Look at each thing you wrote and tie it to a potential interest or career sign. For Example:
- Nature Lover - A job in ecology or an activist
- Leader - Management or starting your own business
- Solo Go Getter - A job where you can work alone as an entrepreneur
- Performer - An actor, singer, or dancer

2) Circle the ones that speak to you the most.

3) Now do the same thing for things you're now interested in and the characteristics you portray. It can be helpful to ask friends and family if you're drawing blanks.

4) Again, tie these things to potential career choices or career circumstances that may relate to each listed item you're interested in now.

5) Circle the ones that speak to you the most.

6) Write down 10 people who inspire the absolute crap out of you and why. Then write down what it is they do that gets your blood pulsing like liquid confetti.

7) Circle any of these characteristics or jobs that may also appeal to you.

8) From all your data, circle the top 5 careers or job characteristics that appeal to you most and do some research on them. If you can, volunteer for or talk to someone in these fields.

9) Start setting goals related to those jobs or careers and testing the waters to see if they are a right match for you.

10) Chase your new dream career.

Keep coming back to your list until you find something that makes you so inspired you can't sit still, or gives you the support and structure you need in order to do the things you love in your leisure time. When you find it, you'll know.

#FEEL 21

I'M ANXIOUS ABOUT THE FUTURE

It can be hard not to get locked into the worry and fear of what the future might hold. It can be anything from the fear of not having enough time, not doing the thing we love most, the unknown aspect of it all, or the changes it may bring. There's an endless rabbit hole we can jump down when it comes to worrying about the future, whether it be tomorrow or ten years from now. There is no magic answer I can write here that will make that fade because there is no way of knowing what the future holds.

Everyday our paths change with each decision and action we make. That is the beauty of it all, whatever you fear is possible, but so is the complete opposite, and in some ways, we do have an input in how our future unfolds. How? By focusing on the now. There is no magic crystal ball that will tell us our future, but what we do have is right in front of us. This moment, this hour, this day. The only way to rid ourselves of the anxiety that comes with worrying about the future is to check ourselves fully into the present.

Where are you right now? What are you doing? Who are you with? What are you wearing? What time is it? How old are you? Where were you this time last year? How has your life improved? What have you learned since then?

Life can only be lived forwards but understood backwards. There is no understanding or predicting the future, there is just getting there and looking back to understand how you got there. Here in this moment, you will never get this back again. With each ticking second you spend worrying about the future, you rob yourself of the chance to feel connected and content with exactly where you are now. Think of the future like this: there is a long path ahead of you but you're walking at night. You can only see as far as your eyes let you and you can only roughly predict the next few days or weeks, so stop filling your body with all that stress and anxiety.

Trust your path is full of amazing destinations and people jumping in and out along the way. Check back into the right now. Live this moment to its fullest so that you don't waste an inch of walkway. Taste your foods, appreciate the things you have, spend time with the people around you, do your best at work or school, and give some time to yourself as well. The rest of your life will figure itself out as you do, but if we check into the moment and appreciate it at its fullest, we stop trying to be in two places at once and instead enjoy the journey. And that, my friends, is the key to happiness.

DREAMS, INSPIRATION, & MOTIVATION

#FEEL 22

NO MATTER WHAT I'LL FAIL

Bullshit.

I'm sorry, but bull-friggen-shit. If you go into everything with a defeated attitude, guess what you'll get... defeat. How on earth do you expect to accomplish anything if you go into it already assuming you're a failure? I'm sorry if that's harsh, but you and I both know what this really is. The safety of going into everything assuming the worst gives us the self-righteous feeling of "AH-HA! I knew it." or "told ya so!" anytime something really does go wrong. It's the safety net of always assuming the worst, so that we don't have to actually put in our full 100% or invest our emotions in case we end up disappointed. If we already predict the loss, then we cushion the blow, but what kind of life is that? Any time you go into anything with the mindset of:

- "I will fail"
- "I'm not good enough."
- "Nothing ever works out for me."
- "I don't have it in me."

we instantly set ourselves up for failure because we have already accepted the outcome.

#FEEL22

I'm here to tell you that you can refuse it. Refuse failure. Have the audacity to believe in yourself and your abilities. Tell yourself you can have it, you can do it, and you just might find yourself accomplishing exactly what you thought you never could or having exactly what you thought would never be yours. It could be success, money, your soul mate, good grades, a healthy bod, whatever it is that you're telling yourself you can't or won't have. Stop these thoughts in their tracks. Change your mind and believe you can. I don't mean some half-assed "ok sure, maybe I can". I mean seriously picture yourself having whatever it is you want or are working towards. Feel it in your bones, envision every single detail you can of a reality where you've accomplished it, and then full-heartedly believe in that vision.

You just might surprise yourself with how much this works.

You've got this.

#FEEL 23

I DON'T KNOW WHERE TO START

Start right where you are with all that you have. One step at a time, one action at a time, one breath at a time. Move with what feels right. If you have a goal or a dream in mind, break it down into the smallest pieces you can and start there. If you can't seem to think of a long-term goal that resonates with you yet, then start with short term goals. What do you want to accomplish this year? What do you want to accomplish this month? What do you want to accomplish this week?

If you start taking action, the path will begin to reveal itself to you. There is no road map from this starting point to a destination. There is only life and it can be messy and all over the place, but that's how it's supposed to be. Staying frozen in a state of not knowing where to begin can last your entire life. Ask yourself what feels right. Was it the yoga class you took last month that felt good? Or possibly the writing class you had in high school that still sticks in your mind as the favourite hours of your teen education. We don't have to have a huge, lofty end goal in sight, we just have to let our inner guidance show us the way. Maybe you want to get fit by the end of the year, maybe you want to start a business, maybe you want to travel the world, or maybe you want to establish a dream but just aren't sure of what it is quite yet. All of these goals require a first baby step. Anything from trying a new hobby to finding your future dream job to looking up cheap flights to a dream destination are a form of taking progressive steps forward.

#FEEL23

Don't put so much weight on making every step perfect and don't be afraid to change direction along the way. Just start moving and let the Universe and your inner sense of self guide you. I promise if you don't end up on the moon, you'll land among the stars.

#FEEL23

#Feels Game Changer: The Goal-Getter

1. Determine a goal and time frame. This can be anything from this week, this year, or in your lifetime.

2. Work backwards from that goal on actions that would lead up to achieving this goal. For instance, Goal: Write A Book

- Get Book Published
- Get Book Edited
- Contact Publishing Agencies
- Create Front Cover
- Self Edit Book
- Finish Final Chapter

...you get the drill.

This step may require some research (which in itself is taking action) so give yourself time.

3. Once you've broken down the goals as small as they get, pull out an agenda or your planner on your phone and hit three main tasks this week.

4. Just do it. Don't overthink, just start. Get going. Even if you're not confident, even if you're still unsure, just do it and watch the path become clearer with each step you take.

#FEEL 24

I WANT TO, BUT I JUST CAN'T

There I was, staring at my laptop as the clock ticked past the fifteenth minute since I had last moved. I knew I had so much to do, I knew that I needed to get started, I knew that I was wasting time but no matter how much courage I tried to muster up, no matter how much logic I smacked myself with, no matter how much heat I stuck under my butt, I just couldn't do it.

The worst possible reaction to this is to fill yourself with shame and regret for not being able to complete a task, no matter how simple. Some days it can be a feat just to get up and shower, other days we get so much done in a day we can't believe it. No matter what it is you feel you just can't do right now, this is for you.

Step One - Stop trying to do what you're doing. I know this may sound counter intuitive and make you anxious, but staring at a task you can't seem to start or finally pushing yourself to do it, but not putting in your best work may leave you feeling defeated. Walk away from whatever it is.

Step Two - Gain some perspective. Get outside and walk around the block. Get some fresh air. Go for a drive. Meditate. Do whatever you need to do to pull your focus from feeling as if you can't do something and just let your mind roam free for a while. Sometimes we try to control so much of our lives, our brains are begging for a break to breathe.

Step Three - Ask yourself why you are having trouble starting. Even if you think you want to, what might be stopping you from actually doing it? Is it that you feel you should want to, but would rather scrub toilets than work on it? Is it that you've been working so hard you can't go any longer? Is it that you've got so much going on you can't seem to focus? If you can discover the true reason for what is stopping you from completing the task at hand, it may give you a true insight as to where you are in life.

Step Four - Try going at it from a different angle. Is there somewhere else you can work on this task or someone you can recruit to help? Is there a different time of day or routine you can surround the task with? Or a different task that would gain the same results altogether? Sometimes going at things with a fresh perspective and different execution plan can make the world of a difference.

If none of these steps work and you're still stuck dumbfounded as to why you can't get things done, it might be time to ask yourself if you're on the right path in life. Sometimes our subconscious is much more in tune with our reality than our conscious brain, so it tries to send signals to let us know that something is wrong or that things need to change. If you're on the path toward a career that doesn't quite connect with your true purpose, or your surrounding life situations such as relationships or mental health that is stunting you from growing, it may be time for some changes. So, if there's a life path you're walking along, a task you're trying to complete, a goal you're trying to manifest but you just can't seem to start, and the steps mentioned above don't help, it may be time for a serious life makeover. It sounds like hard work, but it can actually be a lot of fun and in the long run, a pivotal moment towards the life you want and the state of happiness you dream of.

(Check out Game Changer: *I Need Some Change* on pg. 154)

#FEEL 25

I CAN'T GET IT ALL DONE

#Feels Game Changer: Priority Plan

Step one - try to stop freaking out. This does you no good when facing a huge task. Your emotions will take over, causing you to procrastinate or just give up completely. JUST BREATHE.

Step two - tell yourself you've got this. You're going to come up with a plan. Execute that plan accordingly, and do the best you can, because that's all you can do. When you feel yourself freaking out, read this part again.

Step three - Take time to develop a plan. Break down each task into smaller ones. Example: Let's say you have exams...

- What subjects within each exam do you need to cover?
- What books do you need to read?
- What notes do you need to take?

Break these tasks down into things that take roughly 1-2 hours

Step four - grab a planner or use the agenda on your phone to plan what day and time you're going to do each of these tasks. This may require a few late nights but that's okay, you know it's only temporary. As you schedule these things in, try to also schedule breaks (I like to break 15-20 minutes every 2 hours of doing something).

You should consider scheduling things like "off time" where you don't study for an hour or two. Exercise time is a great addition as well. Even if it's just a brisk 30-minute walk, getting exercise during times of stress will help clear your mind, sharpen you up, and give you a sense of accomplishment and stress relief.

TIPS TO KEEP IN MIND.

1. Whenever you're about to begin a task, put your phone on airplane mode, set a timer for the length of time you plan to work, and then hunker down and focus on ONLY THAT TASK. Do not think about everything else you still have to do, only the task at hand. Do your best right here, right now, and forget anything else until that timer beeps.

2. Find little things that bring a sense of joy during these tasks. For me it's going to a cafe, getting a decaf latte, using colourful highlighters, listening to chill music in the background, or lighting candles if I'm working from home. Find your mini sense of bliss.

3. You can only do your very best. There is nothing else you or anyone else can expect from you. If you plan and work hard, then you shouldn't put any guilt or shame on yourself on the outcome. Throw your standards or expectations to the wind and just give it your all. Everything in life is either a blessing or a lesson. These few weeks may be stressful, but they are teaching you how to manage time, how to kick ass when push comes to shove, how to get organized, and how to focus. Even if it doesn't go the way you hope; the sun will come up, you will be okay, life will go on, and it will lead you to exactly where you need to be. Place trust in that and then get to it girl.

#FEEL 26

I'M SICK OF MY BAD HABITS

If you're sick of your bad habits, then change them. I know that sounds far too simple, but what's the use in wasting time complaining about them, when the only way to see a change is to get rid of them and develop better ones? Here's how to do it.

#Feels Game Changer - Change Your Bad Habits

1. Identify what habits you want to change -- keep a list of things you do throughout the day on your phone. If you can, try doing this for a week. Everything from the time you wake up, the foods you eat, if you bite your nails, when you drop your responsibilities, when your mood changes, all of it. Try to take note of as much as you can. After you've collected your data, make a list of the habits you want to change and habits you would like to adopt.

2. Ask yourself what these habits bring you, no matter how bad they are. Everything we do comes with some sort of gratification. Even things like smoking and drinking can be a means of dealing with stress, boredom, or lack of self-love. When we realize why we do the things we do, we can stop being so hard on ourselves for having these habits and instead begin to understand their origin. If you're struggling to understand why you have these habits, also ask yourself when they began. Anything going on in your life during that time may have triggered these bad habits to formulate.

3. Ask yourself why you want to change these habits. This will be the golden ticket that keeps you accountable for your changes. When we have a reason for doing something - getting healthier, being more successful, becoming a better person - it becomes the fuel that keeps us going.

4. Come up with a plan. Challenge yourself to quit your bad habit for 30 days. Plan to work out every other day for two weeks. Spend one whole week going to sleep at 10pm instead of 2am. Coming up with a detailed plan with a beginning date and end goal sets us up to actually start implementing these changes into our lives. Keep in mind it takes approximately 60 days to kick a bad habit or adopt a new one.

5. Stay away from things that may trigger your bad habits. Get rid of all the cigarettes in your house, stop going to the bars, set an alarm on your phone for when you want to go to bed or workout, or hit the grocery store and stock your fridge with healthy foods. Set yourself up for success, not failure.

If you can, keep a journal or notebook detailing your progress. Having a running feed of your successes and feelings along the way can continue to motivate you and keep you on top of your changes and goals. Good luck! **You've got this.**

#FEEL 27

I DON'T WANT TO WORKOUT

Sweet niblets, who does? Here's the thing, as much as you don't want to, a part of you obviously does, otherwise it wouldn't even be a thought on your radar.

So, tell me this, are you going to settle for short-term happiness, or long-term happiness? Is 30 minutes of your day really causing you so much dread that you're too weak to push through? Do you really want your health and fitness as bad as you say you do? If you did, you would push yourself to do it. You would let your desire to achieve your goals and your dreams outweigh the devil on your shoulder telling you to be lazy and skip it all together.
Here's the formula of deciding whether to skip your workout or not.

- Did you get enough sleep last night?
- Have you been rather sedentary today?
- Do you have a fitness goal you're trying to achieve?
- Is there another form of workout you could do instead?
- Are you feeling sluggish, depressed, or anxious?

If you answered yes to any of these questions, then get up and get to it. The evil trick to working out is that once we're doing it (and even more so after we've finished), we realize it wasn't near as much of a big deal as we perceived it to be. It's just the cruel twisted trick our brains like to play on us before doing something we know may cause any sort of discomfort - **exaggerate**.

#FEEL27

If we spend too much time thinking and debating something, we use so much of our mental energy and effort playing around with false predictions and decision making instead of just deciding and doing. Your trouble with getting out there is all mental, not physical.

So, are you going to work out today? If yes, then change into your work out gear. Do it right now. Put this book down, change, and come back.

Done? Great, now do the same with your shoes and headphones and get going. **CRUSH IT. YOU'VE GOT THIS.**

#FEEL 28

I WANT TO GET FIT AND HEALTHY

And you totally can. Getting fit and healthy is a goal. A general goal but a goal nonetheless. First things first, define what fit and healthy means you. I suggest trying to stay away from weight and aesthetics. Create your definition based off feeling and fitness goals. This could be running 5km in a certain amount of time or getting to a place where you feel confident in a bathing suit (not that you shouldn't already, you're beautiful just the way you are). The only numbers you want to use for these should be fitness related, not body related. This is how we keep from falling into unhealthy and unrealistic mindsets. Better yet, try not to weigh yourself at all because you are not a number on a scale. You are a soul inside a body who's looking to live their most healthy, vibrant life. Let that be the ultimate goal.

Once you have a goal, it's time to curate a plan. This can be anything from a lifestyle you want to follow (may I suggest vegan, it's rewarding, filling and healthy AF), to a fitness goal you want to achieve (becoming a yoga pro, being able to do a certain number of push-ups, etc.). Once you have a general execution plan, it's time to breakdown those tasks into smaller ones. For instance, if you want to work up to running 5km, pull out your planner and choose three days this week that you will run 1km, 1.5km, and then 2km. If you're already a runner, then you can up the distance or dwindle down the time of your 5km. If you want to start eating whole foods you need to make a grocery list, pick a grocery day, clear the junk food from your home and even potentially meal prep (this will change your life).

The best way to do this is to invest in a planner, or better yet, a fitness agenda to schedule your meal prep days, your workout days, and what types of workouts you'll be doing. It will also give you the ability to keep a log of your times, distances, progress, and even feelings. You can also keep track of things like the hours of sleep you get at night and water consumed in a day. Make getting fit and healthy fun! That's what's going to make it stick. You don't have to do what anyone else is doing, you just have to do what feels right for you.

So, set a goal, come up with a plan, break it down over days and weeks and then make it fun. Keep track of your progress and goals, have bi-weekly check-in/updates where you reward yourself for sticking to your plans, and watch your life change. An even better idea may be to make a blog or online accountability page on Tumblr or Blogger to share your health journey with others. Even if no one else is following, doing something as simple as this can make the world of a difference in your commitment and motivation. Just having the visual progress of your journey and the habit of checking in and creating something fun from your goal makes it even more rewarding.

Getting fit and healthy doesn't have to be dreadful task. It doesn't need to consume your life, you just have to find the right goal and lifestyle that works for you and make the necessary changes to get to where you want to be. When we drop the stigma of how we want to be fit "aesthetically" and start following our intuition on what feels right in our core, we create our own healthy lifestyle that's adaptable and motivating.

We learn to start seeing fit and healthy on the inside as well as the outside. We make our healthy journey about pushing ourselves and eating healthy foods, along with taking care of our minds by meditating (Game Changer: *Meditating* pg. 156) and giving ourselves breaks and rewards. Life is all about balance. You just need to find that sweet spot of enjoying exactly where you're at, while working towards who you want to be. Following the steps above will get you there.

Good luck and keep me posted!

You've got this.

ALBERT SCHWEITZER

"Success is not the key to happiness. Happiness is the key to success. If you love what you are doing, you will be successful."

#FEEL 29

I'M NOT SUCCESSFUL

#Feels Game Changer: Define Success

In your own words, what does it mean to be successful? Before you read on, write it down on paper or in your phone. Get as detailed as possible.

Look at your definition closely. This is the standard you are holding over yourself right now. This is the thing sucking all the joy out of your present moment and keeping you stuck in a rat race. You can never seem to catch up to where you feel you need to be or amount to anything worth being happy over.

Let's get real about the definition of success. To me, anyone who is genuinely happy and grateful is successful. Of course, it's great to set our sights on goals and dreams of making x amount of money, creating something from the ground up, getting married to the love of our lives, having this, doing that, but these do not equate to success. These are mere accomplishments. There are many people all over this world who have everything you have ever wanted yet are still some of the saddest and most unhappy people around. You cannot walk around life with the idea that you can and will only be happy when you achieve this or do that. Is it important to set goals and standards for ourselves? Yes, but there needs to be a realistic approach to it. Success is not defined by the amount of things we have, the people we know, our follower count, or our status quo. Success is based on how happy we are, and as we know, happiness is not a destination, it's a way of living. We must create our own idea of a successful life all while being successful right here in this moment.

How do you do that? Start by establishing your goals and dreams in life. Keep in mind that one person's idea of this may be different from your own. The idea of perfection forced upon us via social media and the majority of society does not have to be your standard. One person may want to travel the world, another might want to grow their own garden, another may want to spend their time raising children and caring for a family at home. Create your dream life and, like always, write it down.

The next step is to become successful right now. Underneath your dream life, write down things you are grateful for that are already part of your reality. Maybe it's your dog, the comfy AF pillows you get to sleep on at night, the food on your plate, your education, your friends and family, the bomb outfit you put together today, the new song you've recently become obsessed with, or the soy latte you got on your way to work. It can be anything. It's important to list even the smallest things because these tiny pockets of joy are the recipe to being a successful happy person every single day.

Finding gratitude in all the little things, including the actual day given to us itself, is exactly how you become happy and in turn become successful. Doing this also raises the vibrations you're sending out to the Universe which will only attract more of these good things to you. This even includes the dream life you wrote down before this. It filters the way we see ourselves and our lives from a place of failure to a place of fulfillment and abundance. It opens our minds to new opportunities, creates a space for kindness to those around us and most importantly, love for ourselves. To me, that sounds like the definition of the most successful people on Earth.

So ask yourself again, what do you believe it means to be successful?

#FEEL 30

I'M HOLDING MYSELF BACK

Sometimes we can become so worn down by the lows of life that it causes us to stop reaching for the highs. We stay in our comfort zones of not-worthy, not-good-enough, or could-nevers because we tell ourselves it's our only truth. We lie and force ourselves to believe these things so that we don't have to go through the hard work it takes to prove otherwise. We do it so we don't have to face the pain it may take to push through and persevere, despite the blows this world may hit us with.

But you don't have to. You can decide to put all the weight down. You can let go of the pain you feel and the hatred inside and shed your skin. Once you do, you'll finally allow yourself to go after the things you truly want.

You can put on your boxing gloves, lace up your shoes, and start fighting for yourself, and you should, because no one else will do it for you. You can raise your standard of life and start climbing out of the hole you're in, because there's a whole life out there waiting for you to get up and start chasing again. There are happy moments that haven't happened to you yet, there are people you'll love who are out there waiting for you, and there are opportunities that will bring you so much joy just waiting for you to come knocking. It's all out there right now, right at this very second.

So, shed the weight, forgive yourself, take the lessons your hard times have taught you, and get out there. Start going after what you want, because even if you can't believe it right away, I'm here to tell you that you are so beyond worthy of happiness, fulfillment, and a life that makes you want to bolt out of bed in the morning. You are worthy of your dreams and goals, you are worthy of the good things life has to offer and ultimately, you are worthy of your own love.

You've got this.

CONFIDENCE/ SELF ESTEEM

#FEEL 31

I'M NOT GOOD ENOUGH

Feeling as though you are not good enough is one of the most heart wrenching feelings in the world. It can be hard to believe differently no matter what anyone tells us, but allow me to try. Often times, the pressure we put on ourselves is so heavy that we make it nearly impossible to ever meet up to these unrealistic expectations. This leaves us with a constant feeling of not being good enough. How do we fix it? All it takes is a simple shift in perspective.

It starts with realizing everything we say and do in life is guided by our subconscious. Even the things we may look back on with regret taught us a lesson, and in life; knowledge is power. Every single moment of your life, including the one you're in right now, is exactly where you are supposed to be. It's just playing into a bigger picture you may not be able to see yet. Imagine yourself in the future looking back at who you are now and try to send that version of you comfort in knowing it will all be okay. That it's all part of the journey.

Imagine the older, wiser version of you trying to comfort you with the thought that you were always enough, and that everything you did led you to exactly where you wanted to be. And the best part of it all is that we can speed up the process of getting there by putting trust in ourselves, listening to our intuition, and having faith that everything we do (and don't do) is just part of the path that leads us through an amazing life. If you want to be more fit, more intelligent, more successful, have more friends, or make more money and can't accept yourself and where you are in life right now, you'll never appreciate the better times once you get there. Life is all about balance. Some days you are going to absolutely kill it and other days you're going to feel like crap about yourself, abandon your responsibilities, and not feel up for the challenge. Both are completely okay.

Some days you're going to eat like a complete goddess whilst hitting up a hot yoga class and getting a morning run in. Other days you'll get a burrito delivered to your door as you resume position on the couch, binge watching a show in your sweat pants. Again, both are completely okay. It's all about balance. In all these moments you are living, you a breathing, and you are existing. That by itself makes you enough. Take some of the pressure off your shoulders. Take a deep breath. Lean into life and trust your gut and your journey. Start filling yourself up with positive self talk, focus in on the things you love and enjoy about yourself, and watch your life change for the better. Start taking action that feels most right in your soul and be conscious in knowing that you are on your way to everything you wish for, all while accepting and appreciating exactly where you're at.

Know that being good enough doesn't come from a standard or an accomplishment, it comes from accepting yourself and the reality of your life. Let go, focus in on the things around you that you love and cherish and start doing the things that make you feel good about yourself. Change your standards of what is good enough and let living this life with joy and gratitude be all it takes to feel enough.

#FEEL 32

I HATE MY BODY

We live in a society that profits from our self-hatred. Hate the way your hair looks? Get this product. Hate the way your body looks? Buy this special program. We are constantly flooded with curated and "perfect" images. They beat their way so deep into our self-conscious that just scrolling past a lounging model or our eyes flicking past a billboard on the highway can leave us feeling like complete crap. These images leave a little piece of what perfection is supposed to look like, slowly altering our perceptions with each glance we take. Somehow this makes us go from being young souls exploring the earth in these bodies - climbing trees, taking naps, and counting down the minutes until recess - to adults constantly comparing how we look to everyone else, trying fad diets to slim our bodies down, and basing everything we have and our self-worth on inches or numbers on the scale.

We so easily forget everything our bodies do on the inside because we're so obsessed with the exterior wrapping. We forget that our bodies let us know when it's time to sleep, heal whenever we fall, take us from point A to point B, give us creative ideas and the ability to travel, explore, laugh, cry, and express our love. Our bodies do everything they're supposed to and we repay them by picking them apart, torturing them with dangerous habits, and abusing them with lack of self-care and love. This will never change unless you do.

#FEEL32

#Feels Game Changer: Mind vs. Body Meditation

Close your eyes for a quick moment and actually feel your body. Don't look at it, don't touch it, just check in with how it feels. Wiggle your toes, stretch your arms, lean your head from side to side and back around again. Feel your heartbeat, count each pump. Take a deep breath and fill your lungs from the bottom of your belly to the tops of your shoulders. Do it two more times. Feel the energy buzzing underneath the surface of your skin. Feel the life in your fingertips and the light in your mind. You are not your body, you are inside of your body. You are everything you say and do, you are not everything you look like and wear.

This is it. This is the one body you get. This is the vessel that takes you from the beginning of your life on earth until it's time to venture to wherever is next. Instead of constantly picking your body apart and comparing it to unrealistic expectations by society, and companies trying to sell a product or make a dollar, be defiant. Be the rebel that decides to love their body. Be the person who decides to listen to their body and work with it to attain optimal health in life, both physically and mentally. There is nothing wrong with working on ourselves to become healthier and more fit, but there's a line we can cross when we make our purpose to look or be like someone else. Your body is your best friend. It is the reason you can live the life you do, from typing on your phone, kissing the person you love, hugging your dog, and dancing the night away with your friends. It's time we start honouring them by treating them right with healthy foods, upbeat activity, cute outfits, warm bubble baths, long massages, and hell I'll say it, even hot sex (sorry fam).

Our bodies are our means of transportation through every peak and valley in this life. Every amazing memory, every goal you achieve, every thought you have, everything you see and do is only possible because of your body. Defy society and choose to love it. It's doing everything it should and was meant to do. The only thing broken is our perspective, but luckily, we have full control over the standards and ideals we choose to accept and reject as individuals. So, accept your body and reject any standard that tells you it's not good enough. You don't have room for that kind of negativity in your life.

JEN SINCERO

"You are perfect. To think anything less is as pointless as a river thinking that it's got too many curves or that it moves too slowly or that its rapids are too rapid. Says who? You're on a journey with no defined beginning, middle or end. There are no wrong twists and turns. There is just being. And your job is to be as you as you can be. This is why you're here. To shy away from who you truly are would leave the world you-less. You are the only you there is and ever will be. I repeat, you are the only you there is and ever will be. Do not deny the world its one and only chance to bask in your brilliance."

94

#FEEL 33

I HAVE NOTHING TO OFFER

If you believe you have nothing to offer, then you truly don't know yourself. You're not giving yourself nearly enough credit. You're holding yourself to a standard you've set so high that you've lost the ability to see your worth and all the amazing things you contribute to this world. Feeling like you have nothing to offer stems from a deep lack of self-love and confidence. (See #feel *I Don't Love Myself* on pg. 103)

Think of a time you helped someone in need. This can be anything from lending a helping hand to giving comforting words to someone who was down. Think of a time you were so into something you were giddy with excitement and couldn't wait to tell those around you. This can even be as small as the macaroni frame you made in preschool. There are so many talents, ideas, projects, and goals sitting inside of you just waiting to be discovered. If you continue to tell yourself you have nothing to offer, it's as if you are placing another layer between you and all of things you could be bringing to the table. The trick is to appreciate and acknowledge the small things you already have and do in order to grow and eventually allow yourself to see and honour the bigger things.

Tossing a smile to a stranger is giving something to this world. Volunteering your time is even bigger. Helping someone in need, whether it be someone you know or by donating to a cause that warms your soul is contributing to this Earth. Start there and see where it takes you.

#FEEL33

#Feels Game Changer: Soul Search Journal Jot

Grab a journal or piece of paper and write down the top five things you enjoy doing most in this world. It can be anything from listening to music, drinking coffee, being outside, spending time with family, playing video games, or learning new things.

Beside each thing, write down how you contribute to it or ways you could.

Example: Spending time with family makes the people you care most about feel good. Making public playlists contributes your music tastes to the world. Volunteering to plant trees helps the environment. You have so much to offer this world and if you just gave yourself the credit and love you deserved, you would see it all so clearly.

SHANNON L. ALDER

"Life always begins with one step outside of your comfort zone."

97

#FEEL 34

I'M OUTSIDE OF MY COMFORT ZONE

Being outside of our comfort zone can go one of two ways:

- We let go, see where the adventure takes us and end up expanding our comfort zone for the next time we decide to try something new.
- We freak out, retreat, and rush back to the quickest places that bring us a sense of safety.

The only way to grow and gain confidence in the new is to let go of any sense of control or safety and lean into the idea of being a little uncomfortable. It's totally okay to be in a situation where you aren't entirely sure what to do or say. Don't put so much pressure on yourself to get every moment exactly right and achieve everything with graceful bliss. Instead, allow yourself to let go and let the adventure of something new lead you. Try not to overthink wherever you are or whatever you're doing and instead let yourself get comfortable with being uncomfortable.

There is no wrong move or answer in life. There is only experience and growth. Putting ourselves in a situation where we're unsure and apprehensive is a chance for us to experience something new and allow the adventure of life to bring to us somewhere we may have never been before. These moments of stepping outside of our comfort zone grow the foundation of where we stand, leading us to new places, and making us more confident in ourselves.

#FEEL34

Think; if as a child you never stepped outside of your comfort zone, you would have never learned to walk, made new friends, explored your imagination, or have grown into the person you are today. If we were to stay inside the confinements of the things and places that felt safe to us, it would leave us with no ability to taste life or discover new things. Pushing ourselves outside of our comfort zone leads us to new places, people, and opportunities that become a part of us, forcing ourselves to grow more into who we are meant to be.

So, wherever you are, whatever you're doing, whoever you're with, try to see this as the Universe giving you the opportunity to expand and grow. If you're still freaked, think of the absolute worst thing that could happen. Establishing this will allow ourselves to put a halt to our overriding minds and realize that in the grand scheme of things, we haven't much to lose - and possibly everything to gain. So, chin up, walk strong, and put yourself out there. Life begins at the edge of our comfort zones, and if all else fails, you can always go home knowing you at least tried.

#FEEL 35

I'M HAVING A PITY PARTY

Might I suggest you skip this #feel if you're a little more on the sensitive side because we're about to get mighty real.

It's time to stop sulking. Sitting around feeling sorry for ourselves does nothing but leave us empty handed and ego wounded. No matter what's going on that's leaving you feeling as if the whole world is against you, it could always be worse. There is an answer to the way you're feeling. I know it can be hard to resist throwing up your hands in defeat, giving into the belief that nothing good ever comes to you, but name one pity party that attracted any possible good outcome. Odds are, you can't. All you are gaining from this is not only your own pity, but soon everyone else's.

Having a pity party is like the adult version of throwing a temper tantrum. We lay down, kick, scream, and sulk until the world (or our mother) gives us what we wanted and while we'd skip off in delighted achievement, we know we went about it the wrong way. If we sit around sulking waiting for the Universe or someone else to come along, fix our problems, and boost our confidence, we're giving up all control and responsibility for our lives. Not to mention we're showing everyone around us that we aren't capable of handling things on our own. There's a really sad reality check we all get from time to time; sometimes, life just blows.

Quite literally, it blows us off our feet and smacks us down on our butts leaving us winded, wounded, and dumbfounded. But what makes us isn't what breaks us, it's how we put ourselves back together that matters. So yes, you can sit here and sulk, you can obsess over how the world isn't fair and how mistreated and misunderstood you feel, or you can get up, dust off, and keep charging forward. I'm not saying don't give yourself time to let the wounds heal, but having a pity party is a waste of your time. It’s in the way we take what life throws at us and how we heal and grow from the injustices of life that defines who we are.

Get back up. Shake it off. Reset your focus and your vision. Keep going and never forget to get back up every time you fall down.

APRIL GREEN

"That's the thing about self-love. You wear it like a dress and it becomes more and more exquisite with time."

102

#FEEL 36

I DON'T LOVE MYSELF

There is not one reason on this planet that you should go around hating yourself. From the time you were born to this very second, you have been the one and only person supporting yourself through every moment. You did not come into this world hating yourself. With time, the opinions of others, the standards of society, and the pressures you've put on yourself have taught you to unravel the love and light you were born with and replace it with self-doubt and low self-esteem. If there is one standard you are to live by for the rest of your life, let it be this; your self-worth comes from the acceptance of yourself, not from others.

We become so consumed with what we believe everyone else tells us we should be instead of accepting ourselves just as we are. When we stop doing things in order to gain acceptance and love from those around us and start doing the things that feel right to who we authentically are, we enter a state of self-acceptance and assurance. We must learn to be confident and love ourselves for everything that we are and stop measuring our self-worth by everything that we are not. Think; if you don't love yourself, how can anyone else? All the love and light we attract in this life begins with the light and love we give ourselves.

This world is already equipped with enough hatred and burdens to be everything we aren't and to acquire everything we don't have. Why add more to the mix? Instead, be there for yourself. Show up for yourself. Promise that you are going to love and take care of yourself so that no matter what happens in your life, you will never go unloved. Promise that you are going to take care of yourself the way you deserve. That you're going to treat your body with respect and adoration, feed it nutritious foods, move it around, give it rest when needed, and let it live freely. Promise to treat yourself with the highest level of care so that no matter where you are or who you're with, you're never left uncared for.

Promise yourself you will focus on thoughts that build you up instead of tear you down. Promise yourself that you will forgive your mistakes and grow from your hardships. Promise yourself that you will try, and if you fail or things don't go as planned, you'll be kind and gentle with yourself knowing that you are doing the best you can. Promise to remind yourself that despite all the expanding, growing, learning, and improving you're doing, at every single stage you are always enough - you are always loved - you are always cared for.

The way we love ourselves is the way we teach others to love us, including the Universe. We must first go inside ourselves to find the acceptance and love we need in order to feel fulfilled and full of life. We have to be our own cheerleaders, our own biggest fans, our own best friends so that no matter what the seasons of life brings our way, we have a support team inside to get us through. Accept yourself for who you are, love yourself for everything that makes up the being that is you, and love yourself enough to keep all of these promises to yourself.

You've got this.

MARTHA BECK

"Although beauty may be in the eye of the beholder, the feeling of being beautiful exists solely in the mind of the beheld."

105

#FEEL 37

I DON'T FEEL PRETTY

I get it. It can be hard to feel beautiful in a world that portrays it as an illusion instead of a feeling. We're constantly flooded with images of perfected women and men and our Instagram's are swamped with "goal" bodies, hair, faces, and makeup. The media sells this glamourized version of what beauty is and what we have to do or look like to fit the criteria. My opinion? It's all bull.

Bo-log-na. Beauty, while it can be considered to be a physical thing, goes so much deeper than the surface. I know what you're thinking - "she's about to sit here and tell me to love myself for who I am on the inside and all that crap" - but hear me out. Some of the most ridiculously beautiful people on this earth don't have perfect faces, perfect bodies, or perfect hair. They didn't spend thousands getting their bodies or faces reconstructed (or if they do, they do it from a place of self-love and not self-hate. Do you boo!), they don't spend hours obsessing over their appearance or how they look, and they don't waste mental effort worrying about what others think of them.

The most beautiful people on earth are the ones who fully accept and love themselves for who they are, and in turn, radiate that love outward. You can see it in the way they carry themselves, in their smiles, in the way they treat others, and most importantly, in the way they treat themselves. They don't have shifty eyes comparing themselves to other people in the room. They don't scroll through social media picking themselves apart in comparison to the edited images on their feeds. They just exist, exactly as they are, exactly who they are, and that is what makes them beautiful. This state of effortless confidence.

Beauty comes in so many different shapes and forms. What makes us all beautiful as individuals is different and unique to one another. While there is no doubt that the Angelina Jolie's of the world are beautiful, so are the Oprah Winfrey's and the Helen Frankenthaler's. Beauty isn't surface level, it goes as deep as to what we hold value to and set as our life priorities. It's the way we treat strangers on the street and help those in need. It's in our wit and our sarcasm. It's in our choices to be modest or body confident. It is in our brains and our knowledge. It's in the way we use our hands to create art, music, and writing. It's in the words we use to inspire others and leave more light than darkness on this earth. It is in the way we accept and appreciate ourselves for exactly who we are and what we bring to not only to this world, but also ourselves.

Ultimately, beauty comes from the way you love. The way you love others, the way you love yourself, the way you love and express your passions, the way you love this planet, the way you love the little things in life. Whether that's your morning cup of coffee, when your favourite song comes on the radio, or a star filled sky on a clear night - these are what makes you beautiful. When you hold yourself to a standard that isn't even met by the ones posting or sharing it to begin with (hello photoshop, we see you!), you give yourself no chance to live up to these standards. Instead, we can take back the power by shifting our acceptance of what we consider to be pretty or beautiful.

Personally, I believe anyone who lives on this planet sharing light, love, and energy with those around them is beautiful. Anyone who takes the time to be kind is beautiful. Anyone who doesn't need to live loud for attention but instead lives because they are excited about life is beautiful. Anyone who draws outside the lines, stands up for what they believe in, creates something from their hardships or imaginations, make others feel good about themselves are beautiful.

Of course, beauty will always have a category set for the aesthetically pleasing, but why only strive for one category when you fit into the whole damn set. Why accept an idea that society pushes on you to make you feel not good enough when you can set your own definition and boundary for what negative influence you allow into your life.

Beauty is in the eye of the beholder, but ultimately feeling beautiful is in the mind of the beheld. Change your mind, see everything that makes you beautiful, and share it with the world. That, my dear, is what will make you not only pretty, but a unique, classy, and witty individual.

#FEEL 38

I HAVEN'T BEEN MYSELF LATELY

If you haven't felt like yourself there could be two reasons. You're either in a state of change or you're no longer connecting with your purpose. When we feel lost at sea it can be easy to suddenly lose ourselves. We start behaving in ways we never thought we would - picking up habits we never dared do before, hanging around people who enable this new numbness inside, or retreating away from those who are important to us. We may even begin retreating away from ourselves. There's one solid question that can help you decipher which path it is that's making you feel out of touch with yourself; are you unsure or are you unhappy?

If you're feeling excited but unsure of exactly where your feet are standing on the ground beneath you, then odds are you're just in a state of change which isn't a bad thing. As we go through life, we shed layers of things that at one point made us who we were. We go from coffee-haters to caffeine enthusiasts, indoor people to outdoor people, eating baked sweet potatoes instead of chicken fingers and fries, heading to café's instead of clubs, the list goes on. Change can be good and trying new things that we begin to resonate with is part of the evolution of our souls.

If the answer was the latter, then instead of going through a state of change you may be going through a stage of growing pains. Every now and then we all lose ourselves. Beating yourself up for not feeling like yourself lately is the worst thing you can do. Regardless if the person you've been lately has been a better or worse version of who you are, it will all feed into the growth of who you are as an individual. Sometimes you need to lose yourself to find yourself. Odds are, there's something going on in your life or something that has already happened to you that's affecting you more than you want to admit. When we shove these problems down and don't deal with them, they seep deep into our core and start expressing themselves in other ways. Something many of you may not know is that I went through a long phase of numbing myself out by smoking weed.

I knew it was wrong and didn't resonate with my core because it was something that I hid. Whenever we hide something, it's because we're ashamed, yet for the longest time, I couldn't bring to kick it. In fact, it got to a point that I even justified it to myself and others.

"It's a plant. It's natural."
"It helps with my anxiety."
"It makes me relax."
"It makes me more creative."
"It helps me get some sleep."

For three years I continued to do something that felt so wrong inside but helped me run away from dealing with so many issues and problems I didn't want to face. Stressed? Smoke. Sad? Smoke. Angry or frustrated? Smoke.

I'm not saying I believe marijuana is a bad drug, because if I'm being honest, I don't. That said, I do think when something becomes a daily habit used to escape your troubles and numb away the pain you feel, then it officially becomes a problem. When you're skipping social events and lying to people around you, it has become a problem. When it makes you feel as though you are no longer yourself or have control over your life, it becomes a problem.

I tell you this because I want you to know I get where you are. I know what it's like to feel so lost at sea that you have no idea what's right or wrong anymore. To feel like you want to escape whatever demons are chasing you down. To do anything you can to survive through what you've come to believe is something you can't face. It may not be drugs, it could be staying out late, sleeping around, numbing yourself to the point you don't care anymore, treating the people you love poorly, or letting go of the healthy habits that make you feel good - anything that makes you feel the slightest pang of guilt in your chest telling you what you're doing isn't who you are at your core. How do you fix it? It's not easy, but it starts with ridding yourself of the behaviours that are getting in your way, so you can then dig down to the real issues.

Talk to someone you trust about how you feel. Let them in and tell them what's been going on and how you haven't felt yourself. Tell them you want to change and even ask for their help. If it wasn't for my confidant, I don't know if I would have ever stopped. If you need to seek professional help, do it. If this means you need to isolate yourself from the outside world for a while to deal with what's really going on, do it. If this means you need to wipe your slate clean and start fresh, do it. Once you've rid yourself of the habits and behaviours hindering your healing, get down to what it really is that's in your way.

Whatever it is that just popped into your head, that's what you have to deal with. Whether it be lack of self-love, issues at home or with family, fear of the future, fear of yourself, past circumstances like years of bullying or abuse, the list can go on. We've all had a demon or two haunt us, there is no shame in this. The only shame comes from inside when we know we've let these demons win and control our lives. It's okay to not be okay. You don't have to numb it out and fake it for everyone. You can let go, you can get a little angry, you can throw a bit of a fit. You can curse the Universe for the uphill battle and write letters of words you never got to say to those who have hurt you. In fact, you should do all of these things. You should do everything you can to get it out of your system and clean the wounds you've left open but hidden.

Then at last, forgive and let go. This step is the hardest. Admitting what we've been doing wrong and reopening the wounds can be humiliating and hurtful but learning to forgive and let go comes from a strength inside of us that we may not think we have, but do. We have to learn to forgive ourselves for getting so lost, forgive others for hurting us, and forgive the Universe for lining up the stars the way they did. When we accept, forgive, and let go, we kill the demons that keep us from living whole and happily. We take the weight off our shoulders and can breathe again. The world becomes a brighter and lighter place, our smiles come easy, and we get back to the things we love and value that make us who we are. We change our course of life and start accomplishing things we never thought we could.

If you're reading this and you currently feel lost and out of touch with yourself, know that it gets better. It isn't easy, but it won't change unless you face your demons head on. You're not alone, we're all in this together, and speaking as someone who finally made it to the other side - not only do you need this, but it will change your life in unimaginable ways. You'll realize this period of your life where you feel lost and out of touch was actually a part of the journey leading you to finding your way.

You've got this.

C. JOYBELL C.

“I have learned, that the person I have to ask for forgiveness from the most is: myself. You must love yourself. You have to forgive yourself, every day, whenever you remember a shortcoming, a flaw, you have to tell yourself "That's just fine". You have to forgive yourself so much, until you don't even see those things anymore. Because that's what love is like.”

#FEEL 39

I'VE LET MYSELF DOWN

It's okay to feel as though you've let yourself down. From time to time we all do. What's important isn't the mistakes, fumbles, or falls but instead it's the way we pick ourselves back up.

#Feels Game Changer - Forgiveness List

How have you let yourself down? Make a list. Write down every possible way you believe you have let yourself down.

Now destroy it. Burn it, rip it up, stomp on it, drown it, and let the ink seep away. Let go and forgive yourself for everything on this list. Then write a new list of all the ways you've been there for yourself over the years. All the times you've felt proud to be who you are. All the things you know you got right. Let these be your focus. Let these be the inspiration you take as you move to whatever you do next. Let this list be the one you hold your self-worth to.

Your mistakes were never mistakes at all. Anything you could have possibly done to let yourself down was just a lesson life put in front of you, so you could build character and be better equipped in future situations. When you start to see your faults this way, you stop holding yourself prisoner by your imperfections and start seeing everything in this life as a blessing and a lesson. Everything that happens to you in this life, whether it be good or bad, is happening for you, not to you. Even the mistakes and regrets you have happened so you could learn, grow, and move on. Who you are lies in how you bounced back from these shortcomings, not how you punish yourself for them. There is enough pressure from the outside world. You have to have your own back or else you'll crumble from the weight of it all. You have to give yourself the forgiveness and acceptance you seek.

You have to look for the lesson and let it be what you walk away with rather than a greater load of self-hate and humiliation. These things won't do you any good. Let go of the ego and the idea that at every moment in your life, you have to be perfect. Forgive yourself for anything you've done to let yourself down and instead look at how its helped you grow. Then, when all is said and done, move on and shift your focus to where you're heading rather than where you came from. Stop keeping yourself hung up on the ways you think you've fallen short and instead set your sights back on the mountain top. You are on your way, no matter your pace or the roadblocks in the way. You'll never get there if you constantly beat yourself up along the way. Forgive yourself, learn your lesson, and then get back to living.

You have to tell yourself **you've got this.**

RELATIONSHIPS

114

#FEEL 40

I'M NOT LOVED

There is only one source that stems from the feeling of not being loved, and that is a lack of self-love. When we find ourselves reaching for love from outside sources in order to feel good, we will always fall short. A lot of us tend to try to fill the void that's missing inside of us with distractions and the love and affection from others. It is for this reason that some days it can feel as though you have absolutely no one and then days later feel as if you have a million people in your corner. What's the difference between these two days? How you felt about yourself.

When we look around wondering why no one is giving us the love and attention we so desperately want, regardless of how vocal we are about it, what we are truly seeking is just a little self-love. That's the beauty in this feeling. You don't need anyone except for yourself to fix it.

There's a reality we all come to at some point in our lives; no one's love and attention will ever be enough if it doesn't build on top of the foundation of your own self-love and affirmation. There may be something going on in your life that's making you insecure. You may be feeling alone or as if you've failed someone (to which I recommend switching to #feel - *I'm Lonely* pg. 36 and #feel: *I'm Letting Everyone Down* pg. 131 after this). These feelings can then translate inside our minds into feeling worthless and we begin to see everything the people around us are doing as proof that we are not loved or good enough. We internalize people's lack of presence despite the fact they could be busy or have no idea we need them in that moment. We internalize others tones and responses as if we are an annoyance to them when in fact they could just be having a bad day. We look to give ourselves any ounce of proof that the little voice inside our heads that says we aren't good enough is right, so we create these truths out of mere assumptions.

Instead, what we need to do is source the reason we are feeling unloved. What is it that's making you feel as if you aren't good enough for anyone's care? Is it that you believe you're annoying? Is it that you think you're not likeable? Find out what it is that's making you feel as if you aren't loved and then go to battle with those thoughts with other possible truths. Maybe you're just feeling a little lost or as if there's something missing from your life that you're holding yourself back from.

What is it going to take for you to love and feel good about yourself and your life?

This is the most important question to ask yourself when you're feeling this way. Meditate on it, brainstorm about it. What does your heart yearn for? What is your gut telling you? What you really need right now is to follow your intuition and take better care of yourself and you'll realize all the love you think you're missing is within. Over time you may have smothered it with self-deprecating thoughts and false truths, but it can be found again. Take better care of yourself, wake up earlier, workout, eat healthy, make time to do things you're passionate about, make plans with the people you love most and this feeling of not being loved will diminish so fast you'll forget what it was ever like to feel this way.

HUNTER S. THOMPSON

"We are all alone, born alone, die alone, and—in spite of True Romance magazines—we shall all someday look back on our lives and see that, in spite of our company, we were alone the whole way. I do not say lonely—at least, not all the time—but essentially, and finally, alone. This is what makes your self-respect so important, and I don't see how you can respect yourself if you must look in the hearts and minds of others for your happiness."

117

#FEEL 41

I'M AFRAID OF BEING ALONE

There is a big difference between being lonely vs. being alone. When we fear loneliness, what we really fear is the possible isolation stemming from spending time with ourselves. We build up this idea of isolation and fear that if we aren't connected to something or someone, we have nothing or that we'll be forgotten. Any phase of life we go through alone is not only some of the greatest character building moments of our lives, but it's also essential for growth and self-love. When we constantly distract ourselves from ever having to be alone by filling up our time with other people, bad relationships, partying, social media, and essentially anything else we can, we end up wasting our time and energy on things and people that don't bring much to our life. Instead, we have to face the fear head on and charge head first into our state of solo-being. Instead of believing that you will be lonely if you skip the party, cancel the "Netflix and chill" date, or heaven forbid spend a night to yourself, shift the idea to the strength and peace you will get from spending some quality alone-time.

When we rid ourselves of the distractions that keep us from ever having to be alone, we give ourselves the chance to actually strengthen our confidence and learn more about ourselves. Time spent alone gives us the space and room to breathe, think and create without ideas, opinions, or distractions from others. Learning to be comfortable in your own company is the key to discovering whether or not you're truly happy, what path you should be heading down in life, and even to just simply relax and recoup. Being alone is not a weakness but rather one of the most essential strengths in life. To be a lone wolf in a world that fears individuality is to be a rebel in the purest form. You don't need to isolate yourself from the world or cut everyone out in your life, you just need to learn to feel good in your own skin, appreciative of your own company, and be happy in your solo state of being. Take this time you have to yourself to explore new ideas, try new things, read new books, and soul search. These moments of solitude are going to be the building blocks to your confidence, self-love and ultimately, the rest of your life. The fear you feel is a mental roadblock and once you push past it, you'll find so much joy spending time alone you'll wonder why you ever avoided it.

#FEEL 42

SINGLE AF

So, you're single...

God bless! One day you are going to look back on these days and mourn the loss of this solidarity you have. You'll have kids crying, dogs barking, dinner on the stove for five, and someone farting in the same bed as you every night for the rest of your life. What a concept; to be able to foresee this future only to open your eyes right back to here. We practically just traveled through time. Think; you're able to sleep sideways across your bed, you're able to leave your legs shave-free, you're able to make spontaneous road trips and not tell anyone where you're going or what you're doing when you get there. You can cut your hair off without caring if he or she will like it, you can flirt around and meet new people only to go home and cuddle up with your dog and lit candles without anyone around to bother you. You seriously don't have it that bad. In fact, you don't have it bad at all.

I know waiting around for the right person to come walking into your life can feel like a slow process when you want nothing more than to share your life with someone, but as you wait for that to happen you have to enjoy and make the most of these moments you have now. Start ticking things off your single life Bucket List like it's no one's business. Hold your own hand, get rid of your own spiders, find solutions to your own problems, and establish your own sense of who you are. You need to create memories and stories, not only so you can tell the next person you love all about your life before them, but also so one day you can tell your future daughters about how you lived a life of confidence and exploration all on your own, and so you can teach them what it means to be self-sufficient and independent. You don't want to be the girl who only comes to life when she feels she has someone to live for, you want to be the girl that lives for herself. Not only will that attract more potential singles your way, but it will also attract a state of peaceful bliss within that you'll become addicted to. Being single is not a weakness and loving it can be a strength. It's the chance the Universe is giving you to discover who you are on your own so you can stand on your own two feet.

Own it, love yourself the way you're waiting for someone else to love you. I promise this single life won't only be incredible, but one day you'll wake up next to someone you love and realize how fast it went and how everything you did during that time led you right to them.

#FEEL42

#Feels Game Changer: Single Life Bucket List

1. Travel somewhere new completely alone. Explore the city and its landmarks. Take yourself out for food. Bring a book to the park. Take photos of everything you see. Talk to strangers.

2. Live alone for at least a year. Learn to get rid of your own bugs. Make dinners for yourself. Listen to your new playlists on grocery day. Have a workout routine. Sleep sideways across the bed. Burn candles. Drink all the coffee you want. Dance around in your underwear.

3. Dance the night away. Grab your best friend. Wear or buy a hot outfit you feel bomb in. Head out on the town. Take photos with your tongues out. Dance like nobody's watching. Break it down so hard they form a circle around you. Kiss a stranger. Give them your number. Toss them a wink as you leave. Grab post-dance-party food. Head home to your string lit bedroom and put on Gilmore Girls.

4. Get a pet. Adopt, look around, ask a friend (make sure you have the time and the means to give your new best buddy the best life you possibly can, otherwise skip this on the list). Watch movies with them. Explore your city with them. Eat dinner with them. Decorate your place with them. Feed them, love them, give them all the love and attention you have and let them become your ultimate best friend and spirit animal.

5. Say YES for a week. Yes to dinner with your parents. Yes to trying that new dance class. Yes to going on a date with the cute barista at Starbucks. Yes to going to see a movie by yourself. Do it all, try it all.

6. Set out to accomplish a new project. Establish a hobby or goal. Write a book, learn an instrument, perfect the art of pumpkin pie, start a YouTube channel, learn to do makeup, save 10,000 dollars, build something from scratch, volunteer in your city or overseas, learn a new language. Set a goal, make a plan, and conquer the world one single day at a time.

ROBERT FROST

"The best way out is always through."

123

#FEEL 43

IN A FIGHT WITH BAE

Fighting with your significant other is inevitable. When you decide to intertwine your life with someone, getting into battles is part of the contract. There's a chance they may have done something wrong, you may have done something wrong, or it could be over something so mediocre and mundane but you're both feeling moody and want to dish it out. Whatever the reason, instead of dwelling on how they are wrong, try asking yourself how you might be. Put yourself in their shoes and look at the fight from their perspective. Is there anything you may have done to contribute? Is there anything you may need to own up to? This isn't easy as it forces us to shed light on our shortcomings, but no one is perfect including the person you're fighting with. Taking the initiative to see things from their side and own up to your end of the situation may inspire them to do the same. No matter what you're fighting about, every party involved played a part. When we decide to only focus on what they've done wrong is when fights spin out into something much bigger.

When you decided to be with this person, did you hope they would love you through not only your best moments, but also your worst? How many flaws were you afraid they would see? These are the same fears and thoughts they had when they first met you as well. Back then, in that sweet honeymoon phase, everything they did was cute and charming. Now the way they leave their socks on the floor can be all it takes to drive you mad.

We have to let go of these little things and prioritize the love and support we have for each other over being right. We have to be willing to be vulnerable and admit our flaws in order to move past these moments of argument. We have to accept and love the person we're with for exactly who they are, flaws and all. If we don't then we are loving selfishly. If you genuinely love this person, let that outweigh your pride right now. Understand your role in the fight, apologize for your part, and tell them you love them. No minuscule fight is worth outweighing the love and affection you have for this person. Wave your white flag so you can get back to what's really important in life - **takeout and cuddling.**

#FEEL 44

I'M HEARTBROKEN

One of the worst feelings in the world is to have your heart shattered into a million pieces, to watch the future you thought you had crumble away, and to feel rejected and unloved. There's a reason people write songs about it, paint pictures of it, and make movies out of it. Heartbreak is one of the most powerful, wrecking feelings we know as humans.

I'm sorry your heart has been broken. I'm sorry things didn't turn out the way you wanted them to. I know it doesn't seem like it now, but trust that everything happens for a reason. If you love something, let it go. If it comes back to you, then it's yours if you accept it. If it doesn't, it's because something better is out there on its way to you. There is no sense in trying to control the loss you feel. Instead, as hard as it may be, try to focus on what you do have control over. We can't change the minds of the people who leave us, but we can control how we react over it. Let yourself be broken. Cry it out, order the takeout, put on the sweatpants, skip the shower for a few days, listen to the sad music, get rid of their things, mourn the memories, get it out of your system, but don't chase after anyone or anything that's walking away from you. You are so much better than that. Instead, let yourself feel pain and then use that pain to direct your attention inward. Let this be a new chapter of growth. Let go of the change you didn't ask for and try to make the most out of this clean slate that has been handed to you. Whether or not you want this person back, the only way to heal this pain and show them what you're made of is by working towards bettering yourself. Find something to take your mind off the heartbreak for a while. This can be anything from focusing on work, your health, hanging out with friends and family, trying a new hobby, or perfecting a new craft. This isn't a means of not dealing with your heartbreak, it's a way of not only taking a break from the pain but also reminding yourself of all the other avenues your life has to offer.

The absolute best remedy to a broken heart: doing something that will give you a sense of accomplishment, such as helping someone else in need. This good feeling will take a bit of the sting out of your pain and create momentum for more feel-good things. It also doesn't hurt to put the breakup into perspective. Before things were broken off, odds are there were things within the relationship that we ourselves felt weren't ideal. Maybe this person didn't give you the attention you felt you deserved. Maybe they didn't pay attention to details about you or honour what was important to you. Maybe they didn't try to learn more about you, didn't want to share more of their lives with you, made you feel insecure or uncared for, and so on. Try to remember the unwanted characteristics of the relationship on your end of things. Ask yourself this: do you really want to be with someone who doesn't want to be with you? Is it worth trying to make someone stick around who doesn't truly appreciate or love you the way you deserve? Even if it hurts now, it's best we get through the pain of losing this person so we can open ourselves up in the future for the right person to come along.

Don't over analyze the reasons they left and don't blame yourself or beat yourself up because the relationship didn't work out. Instead, try to accept the change for what it is and do everything that you can to make the most out of the pain you feel. Years from now you may look back on some of the biggest heartaches in your life and realize not only the strength they gave you, but also the pivot they made in your path that lead you to someone or something so much greater than you could have ever imagined. Maybe your newfound single life will give you the chance to chase and accomplish your dreams, maybe it'll give you the chance to love and learn more about yourself, maybe it'll give you the chance to travel and explore life, or maybe it'll set you on course with someone who will change your life completely and become your life partner.

Trust that the Universe has a plan for you, and though this part of it may hurt or not make sense, it's part of your bigger picture. If you can stay the course and not lose yourself in the rejection from someone else, you may just find yourself better off on the other side.

You will get through this. Let yourself hurt, let yourself heal, let yourself focus on accomplishing other things, and let yourself move on.

You've got this.

ROY T. BENNETT

"What you stay focused on will grow."

#FEEL 45

SOMEONE I LOVE HAS LET ME DOWN

Whether it be for something small or something much greater, the biggest pain we face is the one caused by the people we love, trust, and value most. No one is perfect. I'm sure there are many times in your life that you made a mistake in a state of feeling lost, confused, angry, or sad. Maybe the standard someone set for you was too high, maybe you weren't feeling yourself, maybe you were dealing with something else entirely and the weight of it played a hand in the action you took. None of us are innocent of letting others down and it's crucial to remember this when someone we love has done so to us.

The first thing we have to do is talk to this person about it. If someone you love has let you down, how can they ever know why if we don't have an open and honest conversation with them? Even if they turn defensive and don't see your side of things, admitting that you're hurt and disappointed is crucial for eventually moving on and letting go. Opening this conversation may also give us a chance to get a better insight into what someone else may be going through in silence. No one does anything with the sole intention to hurt others unless they are malicious creatures. Usually, when we've let someone down it's because we're either hurting or have a difference in opinion. Instead of holding onto your pain, try letting it go in order to comfort and help this person through whatever they may be going through and respect your differences. Agree to disagree?

#FEEL45

If you still can't seem to let go of what someone has done to you, then it's time to get a little selfish. Is this pain causing you to feel angry? Is it seeping its way into other areas of your life? If so, you don't have time for that. Time on this earth is precious and sometimes we have to get selfish in deciding what and who we let affect us. Let go of the pain this person has caused you and learn to know better next time. Distance yourself if you need to. Understand that they too may be feeling hurt or lost and instead of letting that energy affect yours, choose to realize everyone makes mistakes. Decide to forgive and move on with your life, even if they don't apologize.

#FEEL 46

I'M LETTING EVERYONE DOWN

What are the standards you feel you aren't meeting? Do they resonate with who you are and the life you want to be living? Sometimes when we let others down it's because they're holding us to a standard that they have set for their ideal version of us. It's not rare that people in our lives believe they know what's best for us and in wanting to please everyone, we lose what we believe is best for ourselves. Before you go on thinking you've let anyone else down, make sure you aren't letting yourself down in the process. Become extremely clear on if the behaviours and actions others expect of you truly resonate with who you are. Be sure that with racing to meet these standards set on you by the people you value most, you're not forgetting to meet your own.

A mental muscle we have to exercise is learning not to live our lives based on the opinions of others - including those we love and care for the most. When it boils down, we know deep in our core when we are wrong and when we are right. I'm not saying that you should ignore when your parents come to you concerned or disappointed with your poor spending habits or binge-drinking behaviour. I'm saying that inside, you already know when the things you're partaking in are wrong. In feeling you've let other people down, what you're truly feeling is that you've let yourself down. Poor behaviours usually stem from a lack of self-love (check out #feel *I Don't Love Myself* on pg. 103), or from a means of dealing with the pressures, pain, and anxieties that come with life.

How do we fix it? First, get rid of any guilt you feel for letting anyone else down and instead focus on forgiving yourself. Note that the people you've let down don't love you any less, they just want what's best for you.

Get a firm handle on the standards you have for your life. Set them based on what feels right in your core and what you know is right and wrong. Establish what you want to do, goals you want to accomplish in the time you have on this planet, and the person you're working on becoming. Getting clear on these makes it easier for us to stand by our own standards and not get lost in the desires that others have for us even if they mean well.

Next, start working on becoming that person. You don't have to change overnight, and odds are you're still going to make a few mistakes along the way, but start now. Don't wait until you feel better, don't wait until things seem easier, don't wait until you've hit rock bottom. Start now. Make a plan to accomplish the life you've set out for. Accept yourself for exactly who you are and exactly where your life is at. Let your actions speak louder than your words. Start making better decisions for yourself. Take care of yourself.

When we are on a path that aligns with our inner purpose and bliss, it becomes impossible to let ourselves down. We begin to see every mistake we make along the way as growth. If we continue to let those around us down while striving for our truest sense of happiness and joy, then shed the ideals these people have set on you. Love them anyway, but let it be known that you are looking to achieve genuine, authentic happiness. Your definition of that may be different from theirs, but as long as you're happy, that itself should be enough for them.

#FEEL 47

I FEEL RESPONSIBLE FOR SOMEONE ELSE

In life we may find ourselves in a conflict of feeling responsible for someone else. Maybe we feel responsible for making sure someone else gets their life together, responsible for the pain someone else may feel, responsible for taking care of someone, responsible for making sure someone else is constantly safe and happy, etc. It can put a tremendous weight on our shoulders to take on the responsibility for not only our life, but theirs as well. Some of these circumstances are escapable, and others are not. However, no matter why you feel accountable for someone else, there is one thing that every single person on this planet is entitled to: boundaries.

Start with this: you cannot help someone who does not want to help themselves. Let's say you feel responsible for making sure someone gets healthy or happy - if they do not put in any effort, then not only are you carrying the weight of their life, but you're carrying their responsibility to it as well. There are always going to be people in our lives that we care and want the best for. Something we all need to do as individuals is take responsibility for our own lives so that we don't put that burden on anyone else. Anyone who refuses to take responsibility for their own care and life is someone that needs to seek professional help. Without the proper education and mental tools, we are not equipped to be dealing with anyone else's sickness, demons, or lack of self-love. This is not selfish, in fact it's the opposite. Admitting when we aren't capable or equipped to help someone, and instead seeking the professional help they may need is doing the right thing. We can most definitely do our best to help and care for the people we love, even if it's simply letting them know that they are not going through life alone. It's never selfish to set boundaries to keep this state of giving from crossing into unhealthy territory. We cannot be held responsible for anyone else's actions or decisions.

We can hope and pray that people find their way and we can be there with a lending hand when someone asks for help, but in no way is assuming this responsibility helping our cause or theirs. You cannot set yourself on fire to keep others warm. We must set healthy boundaries in all of our relationships not only to teach others to stand on their own two feet, but to teach ourselves as well. You won't have anything to give if you don't care for yourself first. We must lead by example. Taking the time to do the things you love, cutting toxic people out of your life, and defining the limit of help you're willing to give is not a selfish act. In fact, it's essential to keep a sense of inner balance.

Lines get blurry when it comes to the people we love, but one thing we must know and instill in our minds is that we are not responsible for anyone else's happiness, livelihood, will to live, or motivation to get their lives on track. We can help as best as we can but ultimately, if someone does not want to change, they won't. It may take some tough love or pulling away and creating distance, but we have to give others the chance to figure things out for themselves. Otherwise they may never find the inner strength and guidance they need to pick themselves off the ground and truly live for themselves. Do what you can to help, but set your boundaries and take care of yourself first while hoping with all of your heart that with time, they will learn to do the same.

1 CORINTHIANS 15:33

"Do not be misled: Bad company corrupts good character."

#FEEL 48

MY FRIEND IS TOXIC

We are who we surround ourselves with. In fact, we are usually a make-up of the top five people we spend the most time with. When we spend our time with people who are negative, we start to see more negativity pop up in our lives. When we spend our time with people who are positive, we are inspired to see the positivity in everything around us. It's a hard hit to take when we realize that some of the people you are closest to or may have known the longest are some of the biggest sources of pollution in our lives. The people around you and even the ones you love dearly that belittle your ambitions, don't clap for your successes, or only sit in the shallow end of conversation have no place in your life. Instead, take a look at the people who support your dreams, congratulate your accomplishments, and accept you exactly for who you are. Notice the difference you feel when you're surrounded by those people instead.

If you want to be a happier person, you have to surround yourself with happier people. If you want to be an ambitious person, you have to surround yourself with ambitious people. If you want to be a healthy person, you have to surround yourself with people who practice healthy habits. It's that simple. Shifting who you spend time with can be difficult and it may leave you in a state of hanging solo for a while until you start to meet people who ride the same energy wavelengths you're seeking. You'll find that it's better to be in a state of positive change than to be settling for a life surrounded by toxicity.

#FEEL48

Throughout your life, you're going to go through hardships as well as life-changing memories. The people who truly love, care, and support you are the ones you're going to want by your side. No friendship is worth it if it leaves you feeling negative and down about yourself. Surround yourself with people who lift you up, and people you love to lift in return, and watch your entire life begin to change.

#FEEL 49

I DON'T FEEL SUPPORTED

It can be hard to go through life feeling like you're lacking the support you seek from those important to you. Whether it be a new lifestyle you're trying to grow into, a dream you're chasing, or a decision you're making, if we don't feel like the people whose opinions we value most support us, it creates a damper on the inspiration we felt going after. An important question you must always ask yourself when you're left with this #feel; **do you agree with or feel inspired by what you're doing?**

So long as you truly believe and agree with what you're doing, the love and support of others is just a cherry on top of the ice cream, not a necessity to get to where you are going. Everyone on this planet sees the world through their own eyes. Our opinions and beliefs are made up of the string of events, moments, and information we've come in contact with throughout our entire lives. This is why someone who may care deeply about your happiness and your success may not agree with your terms or means of getting there. We have to remember that we are only accountable for fulfilling the desires that pull us from within. We are not responsible for keeping everyone around us happy (see #feel *I'm Letting Everyone Down* pg. 131). Sometimes it takes getting there and showing our results before the people whose support we seek most finally jump on board. Sometimes, we may never get their support and approval, but so long as we continue to stay true to who we are and true to what we believe in our hearts, all we can ask from anyone else is to live and let live. What makes one person happy may not make another. What worked for one person may be totally wrong for someone else. When it boils down to getting support for whatever it is we are doing, go at it like this: Ask the person or people in your life to be supportive of your happiness as opposed to your decision. When you hear them confirm that they support you in being happy, then we have to respect them and stop expecting the support for the things they may not agree with.

Instead, we have to gain that approval from within, and once we do, we'll realize we never needed it from anyone else to begin with. If the people we love and care about want to see us happy, that's all the fulfillment we need. If not, then it may be time to start looking for new friends (see #feel: *My Friend Is Toxic* pg. 136). Aside from that, everything else comes from the truth within and all the answers, support, and guidance we need is already inside of us. We just need to get quiet enough to let it come through.

(See Game Changer: *Meditating* pg. 156)

MAHATMA GANDHI

"The weak can never forgive. Forgiveness is the attribute of the strong."

140

#FEEL 50

I CAN'T FORGIVE

No matter how someone has wronged you, staying angry, sad, hurt, and feeling wronged is only holding yourself in emotional prison. I'm not doubting that whatever has been done to you isn't painful, but when we hold on to that pain and don't let it go, we paint ourselves a victim. We may get so hurt and sad that we cling to the idea of making someone feel guilty for hurting us the way they did. We may get so angry that we seek revenge or have desire to make the other person feel the pain they've caused us. We may get so numb that we stop caring about anything at all. Regardless of the reaction, when we don't allow ourselves to forgive and let go of the things people have done to wrong us, we remain weak and controlled by sources outside of ourselves. We have officially handed all of our power over to this person, giving them and their action the ability to control and manipulate our emotions, energy, and happiness.

We don't have to forget the things people have done to hurt us, but we do need to forgive or else we'll remain trapped by the pain it brought us. By holding onto resentment, we hold on to the negative energy from their actions. By forgiving whatever has been done, whether or not they've asked for it, we free ourselves from the energy that their actions have had on us and allow ourselves to move on. This person may have not meant to hurt us or maybe they did, either way by forgiving them we are not letting them off the hook, we are actually letting ourselves off. Forgiveness isn't a feeling, it's a choice. We have to decide to rise above and let go of what doesn't serve us. This includes forgiving people who aren't even aware they have wronged us as well as forgiving ourselves. We tend to get so caught up in daily living we forget the miracle it is to wake up to a new day. Our time here on earth isn't promised nor is it as long as we think.

There are people who spend their whole lives holding onto resentment towards other people, the world, and themselves. They spend each day they have on Earth stuck in the pessimistic mentality of seeing the glass as half empty, feeling as though they are a victim, and believing life handed them the short end of the stick.

When we are stuck in this victim mentality, it's like putting on a pair of glasses that filters out all of the positivity and light in our lives, leaving us only with the negative proof we need to support our belief that life is unfair. If you can't seem to find a reason to forgive, let it be this: **forgive so you can stop wasting your time**. Forgive so you can continue on with grace. Forgive so you can free yourself to move on with your life and get back to the things that bring you joy. Life is too short to be hung up on the who-did-what's and the ways we've been wronged by other people and ourselves. When we stop taking life so seriously, we allow ourselves to let go of all the heaviness and get back to living light.

And when we live light, we attract light. So muster up the courage and find it in your heart to forgive.

You've got this.

GAME CHANGERS

143

GAME CHANGER

HOW TO MAKE NEW FRIENDS

- Friends of friends -- Whether you've just moved to a new city or are trying to branch out where you live now, try going to more group events with friends you already know. Ask to join one of your best friends when she goes shopping with her childhood buddy. Offer up a drink to someone at a group gathering. Compliment a fellow girls shoes or outfit at the bar. Finding new friends is almost like dating, only with a lot less heartache if things go sour. Plus, it never hurts to be kind and pay a compliment to a fellow chicka.

- Join a class or start up a new hobby -- Sign up for the hot yoga class around the corner from you. Not only will your body and mind thank you, you'll also meet a ton of gals in your area (keep in mind it may be best to strike up small talk pre and post class and not mid-downward dog). If hot yoga isn't your thing, you can also try other things like spin classes, guitar lessons, cooking classes, French or Spanish lessons, even volunteering. Look up local places seeking volunteer work for people your age. Even if you don't meet any new friends you'll feel good and look good by the end of all your attempts.

- Meet people through work or school -- Ask the girl that sits behind you in class if she wants to grab coffee and discuss the lecture. Ask the guy at work if he knows of any good places to grab brunch on a Sunday (since brunch is totally platonic). Don't be afraid to put yourself out there and don't be afraid to ask people who may not be all that similar to you. Some of your best friendships will be with people who are completely different than you are.

- Think outside the box -- Break free from your comfort zone and make rounds at a party. Introduce yourself, ask someone wearing an incredible dress where she got it, smile at strangers in the park, pay for the coffee order behind you. Friends come in all different shapes, ages, and genders. You don't have to stick to people you think would automatically make friends with you. You can be friends with the elderly lady next door, your aunt, the barista at your coffeeshop, or even the guy playing guitar out on the corner. Don't be too picky, be the one that's accepting of everyone. Your circle will grow faster this way.

- Make an effort -- Once you do establish some connections with people, make an effort to make plans with them. Shoot them a text or tag them in funny memes (true friendship). Of course, do your best not to come across overbearing. It's important not to sit back and wait for people to reach out to you. Odds are other people are just as unsure about this whole "new friends" thing as you are. Be confident and put yourself out there, set the standard of your new friendships, and make people feel comfortable.

You've got this.

GAME CHANGER

I WANT TO MANAGE MY TIME BETTER

1) GET AN AGENDA. Agendas and planners will save your life. If you don't want to use a physical book or have to carry something around with you, utilize apps on your phone. The calendar app on the iPhone is wicked for not only setting events and filling in time slots, but you can even set locations, notes, travel times, and alarms. It even goes as far as letting you colour coordinate. If you want to manage your time better, you need to be keeping up with your to-do's and making a plan of execution. Agendas will enable you to do so.

2) USE A TIMER. This hack will change your life. Most of the time it isn't that we're bad at time-management, it's that we're bad at actually focusing and utilizing the time set out in front of us. Buy a timer or use the one on your phone to set a duration of time that you'll hunker down and focus on the task at hand. For as long as that timer is ticking, focus on that task until you hear the alarm. When it goes off, get up, shake it off, walk around a bit, dance to a song, then set it again and get started on the next task. This will honestly work wonders on your productivity and focus. This hack is the only reason I finished this book.

3) STOP MULTITASKING. Checking your phone every five minutes, having a full out conversation via text whilst trying to write a paper, getting four tasks on your to-do list done at once - whatever you're trying to juggle, stop. Multitasking is actually counter-productive. You need to focus on completing one task at a time. Not only will this shave down the time it takes to complete each task, it will leave you with better results because you're able to focus solely on what's in front of you, giving you the chance to do your best.

4) DECIDE DON'T TRY. Deciding to do something is different than trying to do something. If y ou say you're going to try to make it to spin class, you set yourself up for failure. Decide to make it to spin class so you don't waste time throughout the day flipping back and forth between going and not going. When we decide, no questions asked, we cut out the time wasted bartering with ourselves and we get shit done.

5) DON'T PROCRASTINATE. Again, use a planner for this. If you've planned to do something that day, just do it. Make it a rule that if it's planned, it's already considered done and there is no pushing things off until the next day, the next

hour, or the next week. Make sure you're keeping your day balanced and not setting yourself up for failure by leaving yourself no time to actually complete everything. If you plan your days accordingly, make it a rule that you cannot change what has been sketched in. When you feel procrastination inching its way into your day, attack it instantly with action.

GAME CHANGER

I WANT TO GET MORE ORGANIZED

- Make a plan - What is it that you want to be more organized with? Do you need to organize your closet, social life, calendar, your kitchen cabinets, your budget, or even clean out your entire existence and start new? Decide what it is that needs to be done and the steps it will take to get you there.

- Make a day out of it - Plan a day where you gut out all the areas of your home that you need to organize. Pull it all out and dump it in a central location. Then get back to the area, whether it be your closet, cabinets, desk, shelves, dressers and come up with an organizational system. One by one, start putting things away again using your new system. Donate or recycle anything that no longer has use for you. Otherwise, it just takes up space. A good rule of thumb is that if you haven't used or needed it in the last year, it goes.

- Set some rules - Come up with a budget. Set a weekly workout schedule. Map out your grocery list. Pick a specific day for meal prepping. Come up with fixed rules that your new organized self is going to live by.

- Write things down - Stop relying on memory to keep track of everything. Keep a notepad in your bag/purse or use the notes app in your phone. Any time you're met with something you know you're going to need to remember, write it down.

- 20 Minutes A Day - Spend 20 minutes every morning or every night setting up your planner for the day, creating or checking in with your list of to-dos, and cleaning up the space around you, be it your home, your office, your car, or locker.

- Use a money management app - There are multiple apps available like Mint, Spending Tracker, Pocket Expense, Fudget, and many more to help you keep track of how much money you make, when your bills are due, how much money you're spending, where you're spending it, and how to come up with a savings plan.

- The 'replace it' system - Anytime you want to buy something new, make it a rule that you have to donate or give away something you already have to replace it. For example, if you want a new pair of shoes, donate an old pair or a purse you don't use anymore. If you want to buy a new candle, burn up the one you already have before you allow yourself to pick up the new one. You get the drill.

- Create a list of passwords. - Take one hour to write down all usernames, account numbers, secret answers, and passwords for all of your accounts on a piece of paper. Keep it somewhere safe and update it every time you change a password or account.

- Make yourself schedules and deadlines. - Whatever goal it may be - from cleaning out your garage to starting a blog - create a deadline you'd like it to be done by, and from there, create a schedule to keep you on track.

- Minimize - Don't over-complicate the system. Don't oversaturate your belongings. Minimize the things you own and the process in which you do things so that you can stay organized and simplify your life. Minimizing your belongings and your routines will not only make it easier to stay on task, keep your surroundings clean, and make clutter a distant memory, it will also bring a peace of mind you never knew existed.

GAME CHANGER

HOW TO BUDGET YOURSELF

1) Establish your monthly income. How much money do you have each month after tax and deductions?

2) Establish your monthly expenses. Start with the necessities:

Rent
Cell Phone Bill
Utilities Bill
Car Payments
Insurance
Cable & Internet Bill
Groceries
Gas Money
Gym Membership
Other Misc. Memberships (Audible, Spotify, Apple Music, etc.)
Categorize these by fixed and flexible.

3) See if there are any flexible expenses that you can cut or decrease. Examples: Downgrade your gym membership or cancel it and start running outside. Start using coupons so you can bring your monthly groceries down.

4) Establish how much money you want to have saved and by when. Create monthly check-in/goal amounts. Come up with a monthly amount to deduct from your pay and go straight to savings. Set this up automatically so it is non-negotiable

5) Deduct your monthly expenses and savings plan from your income and establish how much you have left over. This will be your miscellaneous spending for the month for things like going out to dinner, drinks, coffee, etc. If you want to go hardcore, cut this in half and contribute more money towards your savings or debt.

TIPS

- Use apps like Checkout 51 to help cut down on grocery expenses.

- Spend surprise money wisely. Whether you make more pay than you anticipated, Grandma slipped you a fifty, or you find a twenty-dollar bill in an old jacket, try to fight the impulse to blow it instantly and ask yourself where it would be best spent.

- Start meal prepping in order to cut down on wasted food and money spent on eating out. One takeout meal is roughly 15 dollars. If you plan accordingly you could eat a whole days worth of food for less than ten.
  1 meal - $15
  1 full day of meal prep - >$10

- Contribute to an emergency fund. Any chance you can slip a few dollars into ajar or secret stash for emergencies or unexpected expenses.

- Take the cash out. Whatever you have left over for monthly miscellaneous spending, take this out in physical cash and leave your cards at home. This will keep the temptation to spend more than expected or charge it to your credit card at bay.

GAME CHANGER

I WANT TO CREATE BETTER HABITS

1) To establish better habits, we must first come up with goals. Dreaming big is actually proven to help keep our motivation thriving. Set big goals and then break them down to minimum work/to-do's that must be done daily to reach the end goal. Having the big dream in sight will help motivate you towards action when it comes to doing the smaller tasks that don't generally create automatic results.

2) Change your lifestyle, not just your habits. Switch up your routines to better suit the habits you're looking to adopt rather than keeping your lifestyle the same and trying to jump into a new habit. For instance if you want to start working out, instead of just trying to workout any time you can, change your morning routine to wake up a little earlier, put your exercise clothes on right away and go for a run. Even further, add in a healthy breakfast to better suit the lifestyle of your new habit. See the theme here?

3) Establish your reasoning behind each habit. Have a purpose to your changes. Get as detailed as possible. When do you want the habit to be perfected by? How might this new habit change your life? Envision what it might be like to be the person who wakes up early, eats healthy, spends and saves wisely, or reads 15 minutes a day. When you have a vision and a purpose, it will keep you on the right path to your habit goals. BONUS: Make a dream board or a habit tracker. Use a journal daily to track your habits and feelings or even create a display on your bedroom wall of photos that fit the ideal life you're looking to live and how these habits may get you there.

4) Prioritize your mental energy. Try and dwindle down the amount of mental effort you need to use in a day by minimizing the amount of decisions you have to make. Plan your days and routines ahead of time. Set out your exercise gear the night before and set a specific time to work on your new hobby. When you have everything set and established you don't waste your time trying to decide what to wear, how to go about it, what time to complete it, or how long it may take to work on this habit. This allows us to use our mental energy for motivation as opposed to decision making.

5) Don't let yourself falter. New habits are weak, they haven't had time to ingrain themselves into our state of being yet and we often don't go at them with a full charged attitude. Letting ourselves skip a day or procrastinating

starting will keep us from ever actually making change and accomplishing the habits and goals we've set out for. Challenge yourself to stick to your habit to one whole week. In your habit tracker, take note at what point you feel your willpower begin to slip. Is it the first day, third day, one week in? Is it when it overlaps with your social life or when you have too much time to think about it? Come up with a plan for when these mental slips start to creep in so you can counteract their magnetic pull. Push past these mental slips for one full week and see how accomplished you feel. See if this new habit is making any change on your mental state or overall happiness. Challenge yourself to stick to it another week. Keep creating these challenges until the new habits stick.

GAME CHANGER

I NEED SOME CHANGE

Sometimes we need to change things up in our lives in order to shake up our perspective and set ourselves on a new course. Here's a list of 50 different ways to you can change up your life.

1. Change your hair
2. Move around your furniture
3. Start waking up earlier
4. Learn a new language
5. Volunteer somewhere
6. Change up your morning, night, or workout routine
7. Go on a trip
8. Message an old friend
9. Watch an inspiring documentary
10. Take a different route to work or school
11. Try a new coffee order
12. Start a blog or YouTube channel
13. Read a new book
14. Listen to a new artist or genre of music
15. Learn a new recipe to make for dinner
16. Change up your style
17. Kick a bad habit
18. End a toxic relationship
19. Strike up a conversation with a stranger
20. Start a new hobby
21. Make plans with someone you just met
22. Set a new long-term goal
23. Meditate
24. Go to the spa or get a message
25. Declutter your belongings
26. Live by a new mantra for a week
27. Write down 5 things you're grateful for every night
28. Eat one meal a day outside instead of inside
29. Start doing crosswords or sudoku puzzles
30. Go read or work at a café once a week
31. Start writing poetry or drawing in your spare time
32. Start a new collection of things
33. Say yes to everything for a week

34. Create a dream board with your life goals
35. Try a new meal plan or healthy lifestyle change
36. Complete a list of things you've procrastinated about all year
37. Take a weekly nature walk
38. Start ajournal
39. Change your phone and laptop case and backgrounds
40. Practice a new makeup look or routine
41. Start going to bed earlier
42. Adopt a pet (if you have the time and money, if not, adopt an endangered animal online)
43. Start babysitting again
44. Make plans with your family
45. Plant a garden
46. Learn an instrument
47. Forgive or make up with an enemy
48. Create a fun or random social media account (photos of pickles, quotes of the day, PMS problems, coffee photos, etc.)
49. Establish a new tradition
50. Start a new business, program, club, or team.

GAME CHANGER

MEDITATING

Meditation has been proven to help increase concentration, become less irritable, increase your overall health, and strengthen the relationship you have with yourself. Here are some tips on how to do it:

1. Choose your environment. It can be first thing in the morning before you get out of bed, at the park by your home, in your car before heading inside the house, or in your backyard after dinner. Pick a place and a time. It's best if it's somewhere with minimal distractions and where you can find some peace and quiet (headphones or earplugs may help).

2. Sit up straight or lay on your back. Relax your body by taking deep breaths. If you find it hard to concentrate, try focusing on an object like a candle, leaves blowing on the trees, clouds in the sky, etc.

3. Start with clearing your mind and try to focus your concentration on one thing at a time. See your thoughts as clouds drifting by in the sky and try not to cling to any of them. Let them slide past your state of consciousness until your mind feels clear and calm.

4. If concentrating becomes difficult, try guided audio meditations. You can find many different themes and versions online, on YouTube, and through apps on your phone.

5. If your mind starts to slip, use a mantra to bring it back to a state of peace and calm. This can be anything from the standard "om" to "right now my mind is free."

6. Once you've let all of your thoughts slip past your mind or as your guided meditation comes to an end, you should then try to slip into a complete silencing of your mind. Let yourself think of nothing at all. It may feel as though you are levitating, or visions may start to come to you. Slip back into focus by going back to your mantra. Stay here as long as you may need. It is also during this time that answers we may be seeking in our lives come to us willingly. You can start your meditation off with a question for the Universe if there is something you are wanting guidance for.

At the end of your meditation if an answer hasn't arrived, in your new state of calm and awareness, try looking at the problem again and coming up with a new solution. You may see things more clearly now.

GAME CHANGER

STAY LIGHT

One mantra to always live by in life; stay light. There is not one shred of evidence that tells us life is meant to be taken seriously. The sun comes up, the sun goes down, everything in between is often over complicated by us. You are here. You are alive right now in this moment. The second you spent opening this book is gone and the second that's happening right now will leave next. The time you spend on this earth is precious and not promised. When we let life get heavy, we weigh ourselves down with complications, negativity, and a sense of seriousness that can cast everything in shades of darkness. It can become difficult to see the humour in our bad days, the joy in the little things, and the value in the time we have here. Instead, lighten the load; stop taking everything so seriously, laugh at the troubles that keep coming your way, dance even when it feels like everything is falling apart, smile over your morning cup of coffee despite how busy the rest of the day may be and forgive even the most hurtful actions so you can get back to the joy of your life.

When we turn our faces towards the light, we refuse to let our demons control us. We remain untouchable to the stress and anxiety. We let depression fall at our feet. We become weightless in this life and carry a state of bliss with us that touches everyone we come in contact with. We stop letting the tiny minuscule stresses like a stranger cutting us off on our way to work or the refrigerator breaking down keeping us from living our best lives. We accept that life comes with peaks and valleys and highs and lows, and instead of dwelling on the lows while we wish to get back to the highs, we stop taking any of it seriously and enjoy every moment despite what's going on. We see the blessing in all of it. If you can learn to stay light, you can learn to be invincible. You will attract more light toward yourself and your entire life and essence will begin to change. Stay light and watch your #feels melt away.

You've got this.

THANK YOU.

I originally wrote this book last year not having any clue of the challenges I would face or the many late night hours and research I was getting into. What had begun as a small, 30 paged idea turned into a 100-page-pick-me-up book ready to hit you with some helpful truth in the midst of any given #feel. Fast forward to a year later, I decided to give it the makeover it truly deserved so it was something I could officially hold up and be proud of.

I want to thank you for reading this. I want to thank you for supporting my journey and following my mind throughout projects that have seeded, rooted and sprouted over months and years laced together with magic. I want you to know that you are never alone. I want you to remember that no matter how you feel, it will always pass. I want you to realize your worth. I hope that this brought some of it to you.

Thank you for existing, whole and exactly as you are, all while allowing me to do the same.

Also, huge thank you to Zoë Alexandria for helping me shine and polish the entire thing into new existence.

ABOUT THE AUTHOR

If daydreaming were a paying job, Kalyn Nicholson would have found her niche. Thankfully, between spending most of her daytime hours creating videos and podcasts surrounding her everyday lifestyle to nighttime hours drifting upon seas of dreams, Kalyn has found herself a place in this world where what she loves and what she does for a living collide. With more than a million subscribers on her YouTube channel, Kalyn has built a community of fellow dreamers, connecting with all of them through her words of wisdom and personal trials and triumphs. Between dreaming and creating, she's constantly keeping busy, inspiring and encouraging others to chase their own clouds of calling. To see more of her whimsical world, check out her YouTube channel (www.youtube.com/kalynnicholson), Instagram (@kalynnicholson13), and website at www.kalynnicholson.com.

Interior book design by Zoë Alexandria H.

Zoë is a photographer, graphic designer, and content creator based in Chicago, Illinois. Zoë's specialty and passion is simply to create. You can find her on Instagram (@zoealexandriah) and website at www.zoealexandriah.com

DISCLAIMER

While I hope this book may have helped anyone feeling lost, alone or sad, this book is not intended to be a substitute for the medical advice of a licensed psychologist or doctor. All opinions and advice is based off of personal experience and opinion. Anyone reading who might be suffering from mental health should consult with their doctor in any matters relating to his/her state of health.

Made in the USA
Columbia, SC
31 May 2019